MAL OCCHIO
{ *evil eye* }
The Underside of Vision

LAWRENCE DI STASI

NORTH POINT PRESS
San Francisco
1981

Library of Congress Catalogue Card
Number: 81-7

ISBN: 0-86547-033-2

A YOLLA BOLLY PRESS BOOK

This book was produced in association
with the publisher at The Yolla Bolly
Press, Covelo, California. Editorial and
design staff: Carolyn Robertson, James
Robertson, Dan Hibshman, Barbara
Youngblood, Diana Fairbanks. The type
used is Kennerley Bold, designed by
Frederic W. Goudy. It was set by mono-
type at Mackenzie-Harris Corporation,
San Francisco. The book was printed
and bound by Maple-Vail, York,
Pennsylvania.

For Margaretta,
who wanted to see it.

ACKNOWLEDGMENTS

My thanks are due to many people for helping to make this book possible. First must be my great-aunt, Zi' Carmela. The delicious irony of her existence is that though played out essentially in shadow, her life may yet outshine those more luminous others she once doubtless envied. That, to me, is fitting. I should also like to thank Lucia Chiavola Birnbaum whose invitation to lecture on *mal occhio* at Giuliana Haight's Archeoclub provided the initial impetus to the book that eventually resulted. James Monroe's continued interest, suggestions, and discussions of the manuscript proved most valuable. Helpful comments on the script came, too, from James Deetz and Alan Dundes. For his longtime support, comments, constant counsel, and friendship, Malcolm Margolin deserves thanks, tribute, and then some. Sandy Rauch's impeccable service as typist saved me both time and anxiety in preparing a manuscript under deadline. The help of my wife, Margaret, as reader, critic, typist, and mainstay in times of doubt, is obvious to all who know us. I am grateful to Mia Rowe and Cecilia Dracker for ferreting out anecdotal material and to Elaine Di-

Stasi for amuletic research. Information and materials on *mal ojo* provided by Locha Englehart along with her empathy and encouragement have been invaluable. I am in debt to Dan DeWilde for his skill as photographer, winemaker, friend. My thanks go as well to Wink for helping long ago, before the wine was ready. Francesca Valente's aid in obtaining photographs from Italy was indispensable and most appreciated. Last, I should like to acknowledge the contribution of Jim and Carolyn Robertson, who recognized the manuscript's worth and shepherded it through all its stages to publication.

PREFACE

I think that W.H.Auden was right when he said, "The interests of a writer and the interests of his readers are never the same and if, on occasion, they happen to coincide, this is a lucky accident." For me to say, therefore, when or why or how *mal occhio* first engaged my interest would be largely futile, and not only with regard to its effect on a prospective reader. For the peculiar thing about any piece of real writing is that its genesis can never be quite explained; not sense but nonsense governs its begetting. Even less would it do for me to say why *mal occhio* should interest anyone else. Trotting out the reasons that purport to prove why one's obsessions are relevant—to one's own or to any other time—does little but belabor the obvious. Still, there is that trailer of Auden's about luck, and it, too, deserves its due: that to be a writer is to survive on coincidence, is to be in thrall to the "lucky accident." To be sure, one must be primed; one's pupils must be dilated; but then the guiding of one's hand or eye to the unexpected—be it a book on a forgotten shelf or a new acquaintance with a perfect bit of arcana—shifts to other hands. Poets traditionally describe such loving hands as those of the muse. I like to think of them as the hands of Hermes-Mercury, a figure who looms large not only in the text that follows, but in its preparation, indeed in its form. For while informed by the data of science and scholarship, its form is not theirs, nor is its movement. They are Mercurial. That is to say, they move sometimes quickly and in leaps, and in a way that is partisan and partial, rather than objective and exhaustive. Partisans, they are partial to my own felt experience and so follow it, not as the jetliner follows a radar beam, but as the hawk follows wind currents. This being so, the text goes far with *mal occhio* because once having got caught on an updraft here or a downdraft there, it became a matter of riding it as high or as low as it would go. It became a question of resolving the series of problems that *mal occhio* had set afloat in me. That the same problems would not arise for some, nor carry others in the same direction or as far, is to be expected. Auden was right after all. But if even some of the drafts up or down happen to coincide with those of my readers, that would be nice, as Frost said of ice, and would suffice.

Chapter One

Finocchio, finocchio,
Non dami il mal occhio.

Italian children's chant

Early in the life of anyone who belongs to a minority culture, there develops a quick sense of what one should or should not discuss on "the outside." What one has for dinner, what one's father thinks about church or white bread or the schools or the government, all these are unmentionable subjects for they run the risk of exposing one to public ridicule. During my childhood there was always one more of these, the unmentionable of unmentionables, *mal occhio*, or evil eye.

In truth, the subject of *mal occhio* was essentially unmentionable inside as well, no doubt because it was so fundamental as to be beyond discussion. For what is to discuss? A child gets sick, the cause is obvious —evil emanating from outside eyes; and the cure is just as obvious—someone must *fare mal occhio*, or "make *mal occhio*." Indeed, this nondiscussability may be the hallmark of any working belief system; once such things become fit for conversation, they have already begun to lose their power. Does this mean then that, circumscribed inside and outside, one's mind lays

Sound as much as sense is the key to this chant recorded in Tuscany around the turn of the century. Directed at a woman believed to have evil eye, it apparently served both to taunt her and to ward off the malign influence.

{15}

off the subject entirely? No, in the face of the silence one simply assumes. I assumed, first of all, that were I to describe for my friends a typical evil-eye "event," there would be those (the ones with fair hair or fair skin or fair names) who would deride such goings-on as incredible, backward, foreign, superstitious, or worse. I assumed with equal conviction that there would be others (those with Italian surnames) who, though they would certainly not admit to it openly, knew about *il mal occhio*, believed in it, and perhaps even suffered episodes of feverish madness like mine:

it is going back again. everything is getting smaller again like a balloon losing air except not really emptying like a balloon into space, no, pouring out of me and back into their own things: the tick so big so all around pounding me is pulling back now small into the big ben fat on the doily, the pictures of grandma so far and us on the pony and the brownish one of him in the derby all going back, staying. the sheets touch hot now only the high spots of me, leaving again other places, cool open air places. with the all over pins and needles tingling back funny down to my toes, all the way out to the tips instead of terrible inside and outside and, no, don't think it. the smell i can see in my nose again untingling the red sauce *calamari*, the *baccalà* softening in the tub sour and sweet the *dolce* baking, each one only each again and sliding out the door and away from that terrible red ball all mushed in me over me with the tick and the shouting and the walls dark sauce red and mixing me, growing me, pinning down me without room that won't listen that can't hear nothing then but the tingling chords buzzing the pins and needles pulling all in to grow, always to grow me.

Like most assumptions, however, mine have proven to be slightly off the mark. For one thing, far from being limited only to Italians, evil-eye beliefs and practices have been identified in scores of cultures as far apart as Ireland, India, and Mexico. With respect to Italy and Italians, moreover, there are many areas, particularly in the more urbanized North, where belief in *mal occhio* has dropped off considerably in modern times. Many people from these areas seem just barely familiar with the term as something out of a remote past. For most purposes, then, to speak of *mal occhio* among contemporary Italians is to refer mainly to the *Mezzogiorno*—that southern half of the Italian peninsula that stretches from Naples to Sicily. It is here, particularly in the more rural regions, that belief in *mal occhio* has persevered to virtually the present day. And, of course, when half the *Mezzogiorno* shipped out to the cities of America at the turn of the century, *mal occhio* came too, though it did not always survive the transplant with its old vigor.

Mal occhio definitely survived in my family. They came, my father's people, from a town east of Naples called Telese. A small mountain village with one main street running through it, Telese is like most Italian villages—a residential cluster of stucco houses surrounded by farmland. Most villagers go out to the slopes to work the fields each day and return at night to live and socialize. Everyone knows everyone else and what everyone else does. This is the atmosphere in which *mal occhio* thrives.

In 1913, when my father's family immigrated to the United States, this outward scene was transformed considerably. Rural became urban; mountains became coastal plain; farmland yielded to factory town. But inwardly very little changed. Language, food, dress, customs, all remained as they had been. The entire family would continue to live as one: father, mother, cousins, children small and large, married and unmarried. And with them, and not the least of them by any means, the spinster aunt, Zia Carmela.

This Aunt Carmela deserves mention for two reasons. To begin with, she was not simply a live-in sister-in-law. For it was she to whom my grandfather had been originally betrothed back in Italy, until one day he caught sight of a younger sister, broke with the first, and married the second. Nor could the rejected Carmela merely leave town. No, economics and the loyalties of the Italian family dictated that she would stay, and when the family followed my grandfather to America, would come too, for her whole life to remain cornered in that spurned and smoldering air. This was bad enough: a spinster living with those who did her in. Then add one thing more: she was the one who had commerce enough with subterranean powers to cure *mal occhio*. And, I suppose, if by virtue of nothing more than her spinsterized status, was able to lay it on as well. As far as I was concerned, in short, she *was mal occhio*.

Now here is how *il mal occhio* would visit our family, and I am talking about urban America in the 1940s. Someone, most often a child, would be suddenly taken ill. The illness was typically fairly mild— headache, stomachache, fever, very often fever—and accompanied by no other identifiable symptoms. My mother is very specific about this. Here is her communication about a case involving my sister:

I don't know if I told you about Elaine, when she got it from a customer in Westport. I went to help your father this day and took the baby with me. This teacher who hadn't seen her yet couldn't take her eyes off the baby; all she kept saying was how beautiful she was. No sooner did she leave and Elaine got a very high fever. By the time we got home, it was 104, so we called Dr. G, who said he'd be out as soon as he could. In the meantime Zi' Carmela saw her and made *mal occhio* and said Elaine had it very bad. The doctor came and

{19}

couldn't find anything wrong. Told me to do the usual things — alcohol baths, etcetera — which didn't help. Well, Zi' Carmela kept making the *mal occhio*. It took about six hours that time to break it, the worst I ever saw. Finally the fever went down to normal and Elaine was starved. Of course, you all had them but none took so long. The funny thing was that when you kids were really sick, you would never have it. Measles, mumps, sore throats, and such; Zi' Carmela would do it and find no *mal occhio*. When I first came into the family, I thought she was crazy, but I soon changed my mind.

My mother's conversion aside, several things in this account are worth considering. To begin with, the symptoms are typical: high fever but nothing else for which a medical doctor can prescribe. This leads to the conviction that since Zi' Carmela's ministrations both detected the malady and effected the cure, *mal occhio* was certainly the cause. An examination of the conditions confirms this: there was the woman who could not control her admiration for the child. Now when it comes to this woman, presumably the one who inflicted the evil eye, one might expect to find some bitterness or animosity toward her for having been the agent of so much trouble. There is none. Neither is there any implication of evil intent on her part or consideration of retribution on the part of the victims. One might infer from this a thought process concluding that since the woman in question was a non-Italian, she could not have been expected to know any better and was thereby excused. But since this same attitude has held in other cases I have witnessed, and in accounts in the literature as well, one can conclude the following: regarding *mal occhio*, as distinguished from related forms of sorcery and witchcraft, there is seldom an attempt to avenge or even to go to great lengths to identify the activator of the malady. Again, this last could be considered a judgment on the nature of the world—a world so filled with jealous eyes that only a fool would try to keep track of them all. Be that as it may, the point is that where *mal occhio* is suspected, the primary response will always be not retaliation but diagnosis, that is, identification of the malady as *mal occhio*. In some cases that is all that is done; in effect the identification is the cure.

This identification is almost always done in south Italian culture with the olive oil and water ritual. This is what our family meant by "making *mal occhio*." Zia Carmela would always use the same implements—a wide-rimmed soup bowl, whose fluted edges were decorated with roses, and a plain shot glass. First she would fill the bowl with cold water and the glass with Italian olive oil. Next, while dropping three drops of oil from her index finger into the water, she would bless the afflicted person, repeating three times, "*In nome del padre, del figlio, e dello spirito santo.*" Now if the olive oil were to remain in normal drops on the surface, then all was well and nothing more could be done. If, on the other hand, the oil were to spread over the water—with an animated sputtering in severe cases—then that was proof that *mal occhio* was at work, and Zi' Carmela would shift immediately into a curative prayer, "Let the *mal occhio* get behind you and God bring you ahead." She would then change the water and begin a dozen repetitions of the dropping of the drops and the saying of prayers. With each repetition she would change the water.

What Zi' Carmela sought, of course, once the identification had been made, was a change in the behavior of that oil: from a skittish fluid that spread over the water's surface to one that would form tight, perfect globules. And if, after twelve repetitions, the oil continued to spread, the ritual had to be repeated every hour until the desired behavior was restored. In the severe case recalled by my mother, the ritual required six hourly repetitions.

Everyone in my family remembers seeing this done and hearing the droning mumble of Zi' Carmela's making *mal occhio*. When she lived at our house, relatives would call regularly with requests for the diagnosis and cure. Out would come the bowl and glass; drop, drop, drop would go the oil; and the comforting drone of the secret prayers (no one but initiates ever really learns the full text) would begin. Newcomers to the family, skeptics all, were invariably converted. My aunt, for example, recalls the first time her eldest daughter was afflicted. Following a visit from an admiring neighbor, the two-year-old child developed a sudden fever and would not stop crying. Without a phone, my uncle had no choice but to drive to our house to get Zi' Carmela to make *mal occhio*. A budding skeptic himself, he arranged for my aunt to check the time if and when the child got better. To their consternation, and relief, it turned out to be precisely the hour that Zi' Carmela began her oil and water ritual.

Here again, the point that stands out is that the causation is almost casual. Absent are the dramatic, direct curses that one finds in popular representations of *mal occhio*—representations that seek to capitalize on its presumed and thrilling associations with the occult. Rather, one finds a situation that is striking in its normalcy: someone could not help admiring the beauty of a child. That is really the idea that soaked through to the bone, that beauty and excellence attract the eye, and that the admiring eye thus attracted, no matter how benign it may appear, is *mal*, is evil, and capable of causing harm. Indeed, on the surface, or so it seemed to me at the time, beauty was as much the culprit as anything else, beauty stupidly prancing about naked, inciting all that praise. Whenever one was on display, therefore, either shining in one's best clothes, or prodded to sing or play piano or otherwise exhibit excellence, an uncomfortable feeling arose—the feeling that perhaps one would be better served by feigning a defect than by yielding to perfection. Willy or nilly, one tended to blow a lot of performances.

Only much later did the more rational connections of *mal occhio* to jealousy or envy become clear. When people admire what you have, so the explanation went, it means that consciously or not they want what you have, or wish they had it. Lacking that, they would like what you have to be diminished in some way. In due course, albeit mysteriously, all that wishing somehow concentrates in eyes, evil eyes that cannot help but make one sick. Among Italians, of course, where children are at the center of the culture, to be everywhere coddled, cuddled, kissed, pinched, spoiled, and admired, it is children who are most vulnerable to such eyes. Thus, children are most often stricken. And most dangerous to children are the eyes of those who are disappointed with respect to offspring, spinsters, for example. Though I am not sure whether Zi' Carmela herself was considered dangerous on this ground, it seems she should have been a prime suspect.

Dangerous or not, people *will* admire children. One of the precautions that people within an evil-eye culture are expected to take, therefore, is to always, always accompany their praise with some disclaimer. The most common of these in Italian culture is "*Benedica!*" or "*Dio benedica!*" which means "God bless you." In truth, until recently I did not associate *benedica* with *mal occhio* since I heard it used most often to comment on the appetite of a child who had just eaten everything in sight: "*Benedica!*" Its relation to evil eye became apparent only when I learned that people nearly everywhere believe that the glance of a hungry guest can poison food, that is, by means of evil eye. One never eats in front of someone, therefore, without insisting that he partake of some food. Conversely, one never praises a child's appetite without the disclaimer "*Benedica!*"—and this for me became the equivalent of "What an appetite!"

This practice of the ritual disclaimer is extremely important and widespread in evil-eye cultures. Its forms vary from a simple "*Gesundheit!*" to ritual spitting. The general meaning one seeks to convey is "nothing bad intended," that is, by the praise. The Yiddish expression "*Kein ayin nha hara zol Ihm nit schatten*" reveals the original intent most clearly: "An evil eye should not befall him." If someone fails to say "*Benedica*," of course, it is another matter. Then *mal occhio* is definitely threatened. Prudence in such a case dictates that mother or father or guardian make some kind of prophylactic gesture or sign, such as clutching an amulet beneath the dress or in the pocket. But always secretly. Rarely is it deemed advisable to do such a thing in the open, or to confront someone for not saying the blessing. That would be to impute to the offender possession of an evil eye, intentional or not. This is normally considered a grave insult and may turn out to be dangerous besides. No, the thing to do is to have protection, to watch out, and to say the appropriate things. One can never be too careful.

Even so, one cannot always avoid the eye. My mother tells of another time when she was walking her four-year-old niece and some strangers stopped to admire the little girl. No sooner had they passed by than the child began to complain that her legs hurt. When the pain became so great that she could no longer walk, my mother carried her home. My aunt tended to panic and, fearing polio, immediately called the doctor. He could find nothing physically wrong but advised that the child be carefully watched. When my uncle came in from work, he—being Italian—immediately phoned Zi' Carmela. It was indeed *mal occhio* and took three hours to cure.

Now what Zi' Carmela would say about this instance was: "In the first place, you shouldn't be taking the child out so much; there are far too many strangers with the eyes." Indeed, Americans might carry on all they liked about fresh air, but for Zi' Carmela, as for many Italians, the danger of *mal occhio* far outweighed any unproved benefit of the outdoor life. Then she would say, "And why isn't the child wearing some protection?" For when a child was born to the family, Zi' Carmela's first act was to attach to the traditional gold chain and cross a companion piece: the *cornicelli*, or little horns. The first time this happened, my Jewish mother was horrified and refused to allow her firstborn to wear such a thing. But all over Italy, and in America's Little Italies, amulets of every description imaginable are sold, all originally designed to protect against *mal occhio* (though now many people buy them as good-luck charms, having no idea of their

original intent). The favorite seems to be *il corno*, the horn. My grandfather always wore a *corno* on his watch fob; being the rogue he was, he apparently felt he needed it as long as he lived. As for the children, Zi' Carmela kept trying to get the protective *cornicelli* pinned to the inside of our undershirts. My mother resisted all the way and was able to prevail only because my father apparently lacked his usual conviction about this, a practice that seemed in America not quite as apt as it had in Italy. Still, toward the end of his life when his stomach caused him much anguish, he kept returning to *mal occhio* as a possible cure. Such a belief has a way of hanging on.

I have tried to determine if any particular status accrued to my great-aunt due to her position as "eye doctor," but the conclusions are spotty. She looms in memory as something of a crank; quick to anger; terribly bossy and thereby fun to tease; but formidable, particularly when jabbing at one of us with her scissors (they were her standard equipment and are apparently considered prophylactic against *mal occhio*, there being in Italy amulets modeled like scissors); and very much from another era. She was an obvious problem to the family, particularly as she outlasted all her generation and most of the next as well. Her health was always attributed to her iron stomach, which could handle the hottest of peppers as well as or because of daily doses of epsom salts. Whether there were other, darker reasons for her longevity has not been determined. Such a problem spinster might well have been low on the family ladder, but she apparently had some clout in her day, derived perhaps from the power that came to her via *mal occhio*. My mother always thought she got away with so much—she was suspected of pilfering piles of money from my father, uncle, and grandfather, nickels at a time—because everyone feared her just enough not to want to rile her. They always called her a devil, but usually in a familial way. Still, from the Roman Catholic point of view, it was considered a sin to make *mal occhio*, and my mother was sure that's why Zi' Carmela went to Mass every morning: to even up the account.

In Italy there are unquestionably different categories of specialists for curing the many degrees of *mal occhio*. This is logical, given that evil eye is considered responsible for just about everything that goes wrong; put another way, Italians consider that good luck is nothing more than the absence of *mal occhio*. Even houses can become afflicted with evil eye, for which certain hereditary specialists are needed to make them habitable. Some of these specialists are paid for what they do, but as far as I can tell, Zi' Carmela was not. She *was* consulted by people outside the family, however. My mother reports that in the early days a group of women routinely came to the house certain afternoons for prayer and singing and gossip, and part of the program included requests to Zi' Carmela to make *mal occhio* for various people. After the ladies left, she would continue the ritual until a cure was effected, and the following week the successes were reported. One of the women who regularly came for relief was a *comare* (one related through godparentage) whose affliction was having borne a hydrocephalic son. Her belief was firm that someone had given her *mal occhio* when she was pregnant, resulting in calamity. This is typical of the way evil eye is believed to strike everywhere. Though it could cause just about any malady or disaster, the most common targets were the valued, vulnerable ones: children, pregnant women, crops, and farm animals, particularly dairy animals.

As is the case with most arcane lore, there are no manuals for learning the *mal occhio* cure; it must be learned by word of mouth. There is widespread agreement that only at midnight on Christmas Eve can the ritual be passed on to the one next in line. As far as can be gauged, the knowledge is kept in families: mother instructs daughter or goddaughter or niece, the line being essentially matrilineal. One reason for the difficulty in obtaining more information about such things and about precise wording of the ritual is the belief that any revelation of the secret words other than on Christmas Eve results in the loss of the power to cure. Arbitrary as it might seem, this constraint on the spread of information acts as a substantial barrier to research. An additional constraint is the reluctance of people nowadays to admit to practices that seem so superstitious; more than one informant claimed to be unable to remember the words. Still, some information does manage to seep through. What follows are two variations on the basic pattern already outlined:

N, now 85, came to New York from near Naples. She laughs now at *mal occhio* but when young sincerely believed some people could deliberately will the evil eye and some did it without meaning to. It used to scare her, and the cure worked. She remembers one experience when she was about nineteen and went for a cure. The woman made crosses with her thumbs on N's forehead nine times while saying, "*Occhi e contro occhi e perticelli agli occhi. Crepa la invidia e schiattono gli occhi.*" Roughly translated: "Eyes and against eyes and the little openings to the eyes. Envy splits (or dies) and eyes burst."

Of interest here is the slight difference in the ritual (there is no mention of oil and water, though that may have taken place earlier as diagnosis) and the stronger language used to counter or break up the evil eye. Not unrelated is the further fact that the woman lifting the *mal occhio* was said by N to have gone into a severe sweat while performing the ritual. When asked why, she replied that she wasn't sure but thought it was because she was doing something "against God." Here, as elsewhere, there seeps in the faint smell of brimstone.

S, a woman now 80, from the province of Matera, still practices the *mal occhio* ritual. Her use of oil and water is essentially the same as that of Zi' Carmela, though the numbers vary (she repeats the act three times rather than twelve), and the words invoke the Madonna as advocate as well as several saints. She ends with the following words:

> "*Schiatta mal occhio*
> *E non piu avanti.*"
> "Burst evil eye
> And go no further."

What evokes for me a sympathetic ring in this material, aside from its overall familiarity, is the notion of bursting or splitting the evil eye, in Neapolitan dialect, *schiattare*. As a child, the phrase I remember most vividly was the one uttered as Zi' Carmela reached her boiling point, "*Che puozze schiatta!*" ("May you burst in pieces!''). It seems likely now that the words were a spillover from her *mal occhio* ritual.

Of all the forms that *mal occhio* takes in Italy, none is more bizarre nor persists more openly than that involving the person known as *il jettatore*. Through no apparent fault of his own, the *jettatore* is said to be born with eyes that damage whatever they see. Wherever he goes, he is feared. Significantly, he is usually a person of some status: nobleman, priest (some accounts insist that all clergymen are thus afflicted, particularly monks), king, or even the Pope. Pope Pius IX (1792–1878) was a good example of the type. Very popular and considered personally kindly, he nevertheless had this congenital defect: evil eye. No sooner had he been invested as Pope in 1846 when, driving through Rome in an open car, his glance happened to hit a nurse holding a child in an open window. Within minutes, the child fell from the nurse's arms and was killed. No one suggested that the Pope wanted this to happen, but his reputation as a *jettatore* was from then on unshakable. As one contemporary observer said:

If he had not the *jettatura*, it is very odd that everything he blesses makes fiasco. When he blessed our cause against Austria in 1848, we were winning battle after battle, doing famously. Suddenly, everything goes to pieces. The other day he went to Santa Agnese to have a great festival, and down goes the floor in collapse, and the people are all smashed together. Then he visits the column to the Madonna in the Piazza di Spagna, and he blesses it and the workmen, and of course one of the workmen falls from the scaffolding the same day and kills himself. There is nothing so fatal as his blessing.[1]

Another ruler considered to be a *jettatore* was King Alfonso XIII of Spain. So widespread was his reputation for calamity that on a state visit the brave Mussolini himself refused to meet with the king and would communicate only through intermediaries. Still, Alfonso's eye was reputed to have done its work: several sailors sent to greet him were washed overboard; a cannon exploded during a salute to him, killing its crew; and a naval officer who shook hands with the poor monarch collapsed and died.

Here it seems we are in the realm of black humor. In fact, Willa Appel[2] makes the case that the stories of the *jettatore* are indeed based in black humor and that they developed late in Italy—after the ideas of the French Enlightenment were introduced into Naples in the eighteenth century. Unfortunately, the chaos and corruption of Naples made uncongenial soil for rational ideas of social progress. Thus, the *jettatore*, a rational human being who involuntarily brings destruction onto others, symbolizes the frustration and ambivalence of Neapolitan intellectuals. Their new ideas made them eager to change the world but left them powerless to do so, at the same time making them outsiders in their own culture as well (the outsider is almost invariably the bearer of *mal occhio*). Their ambivalence is even reflected in the style of the narrations about the *jettatore*, at once comic and serious, fearful and facetious.

Whatever the merits of this analysis, and I think they are considerable, the *jettatore* represents enough of a variant on the typical evil-eye event to suggest that its differing manifestations ought to be classified. In my family experience, for instance, the attacks were almost always unknowing or involuntary, activated mainly by the attractiveness of the object, that is, a child. It seems that this is the dominant form. The eye of the *jettatore*, on the other hand, though likewise acting without volition, attacks everyone, regardless of wealth, status, or beauty. And not only is he unable to avoid using his evil eye, he cannot avoid getting it either: the defect is inborn. This does not preclude, however, the occasional deliberate acquisition of evil eye. There have always been those who are so disgruntled with their lot in life that they are suspected of having made pacts with the devil in return for the power to spread malice. Indeed, a hint of this suspicion still remains in the attribution of evil eye most often to spinsters, to childless women, to widows, and to monks (who are denied the most prized of worldly goods). To account for these and other variants, therefore, one researcher has employed a four-point scale that classifies any evil-eye event as: intentional or unintentional, discriminate (attacking only select objects) or indiscriminate (attacking anything the glance happens to hit). Even the most diabolical of crones, even Evil Eye Fleegle can be made to fit such a cross.

Intentional evil. The horned one. There is no gainsaying the fact that, important as it is to distinguish between *mal occhio* and true witchcraft, we can hardly avoid noticing an infringement of the *mal occhio* material upon the realm of the so-called dark arts. What this suggests is that despite its obviously Christian symbolism, there are equally important pre-Christian elements in the belief, more, that pre-Christian elements make up the core of the belief. Indeed, this should not be surprising since Italians, like most other Catholics (Mexico comes immediately to mind), tend to keep reviving and worshiping the same old gods, changing only the outward form. So with the *mal occhio* ritual. The "old religion," that is, witchcraft, with its magic practices and spells, forms the not very well hidden substrate of *mal occhio*, one that keeps surfacing as a sense of "sin" or doing something "against God." Some of the prayers that have been collected illustrate this diabolic element very clearly. This charm from Calabria, for example, needs no comment:

> *Cristo, Cristiello!*
> *Tu sei buono*
> *Ma e piu buono quello.*
>
> Christ, little Christ!
> Thou art good
> But how much better is that one
> (i.e., Satan).[3]

Of course, it is well known that south Italians have always been very practical about these matters, and not above applying a bit of pressure on saints or gods to get them to perform better. The idea is, "If you don't help me in my need, there are plenty of others who will," the Mediterranean always having been rich in gods of every description. The corollary to such pragmatism is, "Discard nothing, try everything, whatever works, including that which the Church calls pagan, is sacred." To be sure, this must be one reason for the many variations on the basic theme of cause, ritual, and cure of *mal occhio*. Each region, each family seems to have a favor-

Sewn on the outside of this homemade amulet from Brazil are a cowrie shell and a *figa* (broken). Inside are probably salt and/or special seeds.

ite method, no doubt proven over centuries of individual tinkering. And for some, even that is not enough; the smart way is to use everything available, thereby multiplying protection, as in the following case reported about an Italian-American by Phyllis Williams:

A woman consented to a psychiatric interview, even though she had no faith in the physician (Italian immigrants rarely did). She did so purely because she was fond of the visiting nurse and wanted to please her. She arrived at the clinic with a large handbag clutched in her arms with which she was greatly preoccupied. Nothing could persuade her to part with it. "I tell you after," she confided mysteriously, and went into the doctor's office. When she came out, she opened the bag and exhibited a huge quantity of amulets against the Evil Eye. She had added all she could borrow from her neighbors to those possessed by her own family. "The doctor," she triumphantly asserted, "he no hurt me."[4]

So much for the power of modern science.

Chapter Two

There be none of the affections
which have been noted to fascinate
or bewitch, but love and envy.
They both have vehement wishes;
they frame themselves readily into
imaginations and suggestions, and
they come easily into the eye.

Bacon

Like many a practice whose origins and codes are obscure, the more one learns about *mal occhio*, the more one wishes to ask. One would like to know why olive oil is thought to work as it does; what these amulets are and why they are considered potent; from whence derives this sickness that takes so many forms, and what is its relationship to magic or Christianity or witchcraft; what does it mean and how does it function—socially, psychologically, historically—in the cultures where it is found. We cannot expect direct answers to all these questions. As with attempts to define life itself, an exception always arises to disprove any rule. Nonetheless, one continues to observe and describe and draw tentative conclusions.

Before doing so, however, it may help to summarize what has already been said. *Mal occhio*, or evil eye, manifests as a malady that usually seems not very severe—fever, headache, stomachache, cramps—and might in most cases be called psychosomatic. It most often attacks those in a weakened or vulnerable state, such as babies, pregnant women, crops, and cattle and their products. (Much of the problem with evil eye in Scotland, for example, involves dairying problems: butter that won't churn, milk that goes sour, cows that get sick; in fact, the custom of adorning cows with bells and red ribbons derives from the need for protection against the evil eye.) The cure for *mal occhio* varies but usually includes olive oil and water in south Italy, and does not normally include retribution against the culprit. Those who give evil eye to others may be intentional evil doers or people born with congenitally evil eyes, though in most cases they are simply those who admire or praise without saying the proper words to indicate the absence of envy beneath their glances. A variety of amulets are said to protect against evil eye, and it is definitely considered prudent to wear one or perhaps several of these amulets.

The amulets indeed are a fascinating study in themselves. Every country, every region seems to have its traditional favorites. They can be found in materials of every kind from gold to jade to coral to plastic, though in general it is not the material but the shape or symbolism that counts. Certain materials do carry a potency of their own, however: silver and gold are highly regarded, and iron of any kind has long been considered a prophylactic against witchcraft. In Scotland, for example, it is an old custom to insert an iron horseshoe into butter that refuses to churn. For the most part, though, it is the amulet's shape whose influence is sought. One researcher's collection contains more than two thousand evil-eye amulets from all over the world, and they do not exhaust the types. There are scissors and teeth and silver rings; there are horns of every kind, and knots and braids and bells and seahorses and keys and fish. Garlic is a great protector, as is salt. In Italy, the figure of a male hunchback called *il gobbo* has always been considered potent protection.

Great though the variety of amulets may be, Italians have always favored *il corno*, the horn. Horns come in several shapes and sizes, made of anything from gold to bone. They can be worn on a chain about the neck or attached to charm bracelets or key chains or undershirts. The modern ones found in America's Little Italies are as often as not made of bright red plastic and appear to be a blend of the horn and the chili pepper; it has even been suggested that Italian-

The hunchback combines contradictory qualities. A product of misfortune himself, he brings good luck when cast as an amulet, or in person when one touches his hump. Note, too, the other shapes added for insurance: horseshoe, *mano cornuta*, and chili-corno.

The *cimaruta*, or sprig of rue. This Italian amulet, nearly identical to those found by Frederick Elworthy and E. Neville-Rolfe near Naples in the 1890s, combines several powerful protectors against *mal occhio*: rue, the *mano fica*, the eagle, the cock, the half-moon sacred to Diana, the lotus blossom, the heart, and the key.

The siren with twin fishtails, common as an amulet near Naples, suggests the goddess Diana.

Americans have made a sort of parody of the original *corni*, preferring their modern chili-cornos plastic and toylike rather than solid and serious. As such, they are considered ethnic good-luck charms rather than protective amulets, more pop-culture emblems than cultic symbols.[5]

The traditional *corni*, on the other hand, were the most powerful of talismans against the threat of *mal occhio*. Anything that even looked like a horn—teeth, rooster spurs, crab claws—was, simply by nature of its hornlike quality, effective. In many parts of Italy, in fact, the word *corno* applies to all *mal occhio* amulets as a generic term. The mere mention of the word is considered protection against *mal occhio*. When one is caught without an amulet and suspects an attack, making the sign of the horn with the hand, the "*mano cornuta*," will afford protection as well.

If the phallic nature of these horn amulets and gestures were not obvious enough, one only needs to consider what the Romans employed as evil-eye protection. Priapus was a phallic Roman god who was also known as Fascinus. "Fascination" is itself another name for the evil eye; thus, in Latin, the word *fascinum* may mean "fascination by evil eye" as well as "phallus." With the etymology so clear, the Romans apparently felt no need to disguise the

The *mano fica* (*fico* in Italian means fig; *fica* carries the more earthy meaning, female genitals), called a *figa* in Latin America. The gesture the amulet represents (as well as the act the gesture represents) dates from ancient times.

amulets they wore—obvious phalli in gold and silver hung about the necks of those who wanted protection from evil eye. Anyone who visits Pompeii will run into numerous guides who will indirectly confirm this Roman practice. For a price these leering cicerones will open the locked murals that depict Pompeians with mammoth phalli on display, and these are not so much ancient pornography as charms against the evil eye. The phallic gesture, then, *il corno*, *mano fica*, *mano cornuta*, even, in a pinch, the expedient of grasping one's genitals to ward off suspected fascination, seems to be the chief antidote to *mal occhio*.

Another antidote commonly used against evil eye is spittle. I first heard of this from my mother, who was born in Hungary. When her mother suspected that a child had been hit by evil eye, she would lick the child's eyelids, spit away, and then dry the baby's eyes with the inside of her undershirt (curious, this inside of the undershirt business). Elsewhere, belief in the efficacy of spittle is almost as old as recorded history: Assyrian texts mention spittle as a cure for bad eyes. Egyptian mythology records that the god Thoth restored the eye of Horus by spitting on it. Christ, too, is reported to have used spittle to cure a blind man. More recently, a nineteenth-century Italian formula employs spittle and milk as an eyewash for eye disease. That the efficacy of spittle is in some way connected to the primitive idea that it embodies a person's spirit or essential substance seems reasonable, but the precise relationship to evil eye remains controversial.* Suffice it to say for the moment that spitting on the ground, spitting after a suspected fascinator, or even spitting three times on oneself as in modern Greece are all considered effective protection against evil eye.

Like the relationship of spittle to evil eye, the connection between olive oil and the *mal occhio* ritual has been not altogether clear. Of course, the efficacy of olive oil in a land where it is a food as basic as bread may be as simple as that. People tend to use the materials near at hand: the hunter uses and deifies his prey; the planter uses and deifies corn or wheat. Likewise, since Italians use olive oil to cook, they use olive oil to cure as well. Perhaps. But perhaps there is more.

As we have seen, the olive oil and water ritual functioned in two ways. As diagnosis for one. If the drops of olive oil were to spread over the water, mix with the water, then there was *mal occhio*. Now according to some investigators, that is as far as it goes: the identification *is* the cure. In the ritual that my great-aunt practiced,

*Alan Dundes in a recent article, "Wet and Dry, the Evil Eye," relates the efficacy of spittle to the ancient conception, elucidated by R. B. Onians in *The Origins of European Thought,* that the life-stuff in the body is liquid or fluid. Therefore, the key fluids—fat or marrow, sperm, milk, spittle—are signs and purveyors of life; when they dry up, there is sickness, old age, and death. Spitting in the face of the evil-eye threat is equivalent, according to this view, to countering the drying effect of evil eye with the fluid of life, spittle, which is in effect the generative fluid or its analogue.[6] Howard F. Stein takes a more psychodynamic approach (see page 52).

however, there was the further step that consisted of a dozen repetitions of the dropping of drops and saying of prayers until the cure was effected. The cure was indicated by the olive oil holding once more in globules; that is, it no longer mixed with the water. This brings to mind some folk wisdom about oil and water, to the effect that oil and water do not mix. With respect to *mal occhio*, this could be taken as the normal turn of events, the abnormal being when oil and water *do* mix.

I would submit, however, that the symbolism goes deeper than that. In a typically complex passage in his book *The Psychology of the Transference*, Carl Jung makes several observations that are quite relevant here. Interpreting an illustration from the *Rosarium Philosophorum*, one of the alchemical texts that he found so revelatory, Jung gives us this passage: ". . . life is soul, that is, *oil and water*."[7] Further on we are told that this oil and water combination, the soul, represents Mercurius, or Mercury, the hermaphroditic Roman god whose multivaried nature endeared him to the alchemists, and whose many names include *aqua permanens*, water, and *unctuosum*, oil. Now what Jung makes of this is that in order for there to be life, according to the alchemists, the basic substances of the universe, spirit and matter, have to be joined through the medium of the animating entity, the soul, which is Mercurius, which is oil and water. The soul, in other words, is the *vinculum*, or link between the opposites, body and spirit. And since the psyche* is the modern equivalent of the soul, Jung concludes:

Thus the underlying idea of the psyche proves it to be a half bodily, half spiritual substance, an *anima media natura*, as the alchemists call it, an hermaphroditic being capable of uniting the opposites.[8]

Jung also points out that the use of oil and water in the Catholic sacrament of baptism clearly alludes to this same symbolism.

In applying this symbolism to the *mal occhio* ritual, I think we can infer a thought process like the following. The normal relationship of oil and water is one of paradox and tension—the oil remains in globules that float upon the water, on it but not of it, whole and unmixed. This would appear to symbolize the healthy tension of life, a tension between spirit and matter, which are likewise separate yet connected, in conflict yet mediated or held together by the soul. But when there is sickness (and I gather that the sickness may be mental as well as physical, if indeed there is any difference), the connecting link, and thereby the tension, is somehow lost. This condition is symbolized by the

*The Greek word "psyche" ($\psi\upsilon\chi\eta$), of course, referred to the soul. In his book *The Origins of European Thought*, Onians makes clear that olive oil was considered by both Greeks and Romans to be the vegetable equivalent of soul-stuff in humans, which was primarily centered in the fat or marrow of the br_in and spinal column. Rubbing the body with olive oil was thus a way to restore strength, that is, soul-stuff or psyche. The use of olive oil as a soul symbol in the *mal occhio* ritual thus makes eminent sense.

spreading, skidding mixis that occurs when the oil is dropped into the water. It signifies breakdown and *mal occhio*. As Jung quotes Heraclitus: "It is death for souls to become water."[9] As applied to *mal occhio*, I take this to mean that either spirit is overwhelmed by matter (physical ailment) or matter is overwhelmed by spirit (mental ailment). In either case, and it reminds one of the collapse of cell walls in critical illness, the balanced tension of life is thrown into dissolution. The animating link is gone. As primitive peoples often put it, an ill or insane person is one who has experienced soul loss.

What I would suggest, consequently, is that the condition known as *mal occhio* refers to and derives from a similar ancient conception of soul absence or loss.* As diagnosis, the behavior of oil when cast upon water indicates this condition. To cure the condition one must perform a ritual that induces the oil to return to its tensile or globular state, thereby symbolizing wholeness and the restored link. Of course, with respect to the why of the cure—why ritual dropping of olive oil and prayer should cause the oil to hold and a fever to break— we are in the realm of homeopathic magic. Which some will call faith, or coincidence, or sleight of hand, or the placebo effect. Or some as yet unperceived core of truth.

*See page 74 for a more extensive discussion of this idea as it regards the Mexican custom of tying a red string around a child's wrist or ankle (to bind or tether the soul) to prevent *mal ojo*.

Jung also notes that the soul, that hermaphroditic entity said to unite spirit and matter, "is never complete in the individual unless related to another individual. The unrelated human being lacks wholeness."[10] In what follows, it will be seen that from a different perspective, a more societal perspective, the condition known as *mal occhio* likely refers to this unrelatedness as well. For the threat of *mal occhio* may also be viewed as a mechanism to keep the members of village society related in the same way that spirit, matter, and soul are related. In the homeopathic thinking of early peoples, man is a microcosm of the larger macrocosm of society.

We have seen that the emotion most often related to evil eye is envy, sometimes loosely referred to as jealousy (envy normally means the desire for what someone else has; jealousy is its obverse and refers to an overprotectiveness about what one already has—in effect, fear of others' envy). Etymology confirms this centrality: the Latin word for envy is *invidia*, and in Italy evil eye is sometimes known as *invidia*; the same apparently holds in Hebrew. Too, most people suspected of harboring evil eyes are those who, for reasons of deprivation or low status or poverty, might be expected to be envious: monks, childless women, widows.

It is not surprising, therefore, that most scholarly explanations of evil eye begin with envy. Several recent discussions have attempted to diagram the social dynamics of envy as it operates in peasant societies. The theory goes something like this: life for peasants in the small villages they usually inhabit is said to be a "zero-sum game" in which the amount of goods available to them (not, of course, to the wealthy few who rule) is limited to the point of being virtually static. Thus, what any one person has or gets seriously affects the amount left for his neighbors; there is only so much to go round. One study of a Greek village,[11] for example, applied this analysis very graphically to relations between the sexes. Virgins in the village are considered the most desirable of marriage partners, particularly as the wedding sheets are routinely displayed after the wedding night and must be red stained to confirm virginity. This being the case, anyone who succeeds in getting to a virgin—either publicly in marriage or illicitly—automatically reduces the number of virgins available to others. Competition among males is thus intense to penetrate the citadel, as it were. When someone does, and celebrates his nuptial success in public, he and his bride are automatically in a visible and thereby precarious position: envious eyes are likely to attack.

Alan Dundes (cited earlier) applies this same concept to the competition over liquid or life-stuff. He cites the widespread folk idea that there is only so much liquid to go round and that it is critical to life. Therefore, what one person gets of this life-liquid (it may manifest as wine, sperm, spittle) seriously depletes what is left for others. Hence comes the fear that others desire, via evil eye, one's life-liquid. Hence the widespread custom, when drinking wine, of saluting the other person's health. This latter, like spitting, assures that one has no designs on another's liquid, which otherwise would manifest as *mal occhio*—a drying up of liquid to make him sick (Latin *siccus* means "dry").

In villages all over the Mediterranean the same competition applies to all goods. Whatever one person gets, particularly to excess, deprives someone else; the begetter is thus subject to attacks of envy, and thereby the evil eye. This is not all as bad as it seems, however. In a sense, evil eye, like witchcraft, can be said to operate as a mechanism of social control. It maintains a kind of balance or enforced equality among people who are forced to live in a precarious situation. By its constant presence the

The dominant motif on this pitcher from Orvieto, Italy (c. 6th century B.C.), is the pair of *askoi*, or sacs, which serve as apotropaic eyes. They were presumably meant to guard the pitcher's contents from contamination by evil eye. Similar eyes can be found on many Attic vases and cups.

threat of evil eye tends to control any excessive accumulation of goods and tends to keep runaway egos in check as well. In addition, it provides for a time-honored way of venting one's aggressions, one that is less disruptive than the fights, knifings, feuds, and poisonings that might otherwise occur more often in such close quarters. That, in brief, is the sociologists' theory.

Still, if envy is a good explanation of the social dynamics of evil eye, it remains to find a deeper, structural account of some of its origins in the human psyche. A recent essay by Howard Stein on evil eye among Slovak-Americans is, I think, a fertile attempt to do just that.[12] To comprehend his argument, it is necessary to know something about Slovak child-rearing practices as they relate to evil eye. According to Stein, children in Slovak culture are weaned between the ages of nine months and two years, precisely at the time when teething is hardest. As if these two trials were not enough, Slovak peoples traditionally begin severe toilet training at the same time. It is at this stage of development that evil eye apparently has its origins in this culture. Here is how one of Stein's informants describes it:

I don't know what's truth. Those kind of people — get jealous of you — that you have something. They say baby get evil eye if mother go back nurse the child after she take him off breast, nine to twelve months. When baby cry—went back and nursed it more. Then that child has bad eyes. You never say, "That's nice" (about the baby) because it will turn bad. A fellow had beautiful oxes—he was taking them to sell at market. Another fellow came up the road and say to him, "That's nice oxes you have." The yoke broke the oxes in two! He don't mean it —don't want to do it. It's his eyes. Spit first and then say what you want. When you wean your baby, *don't ever go back!* Finished! Done! No matter how much it cries.[13]

All the elements we have already seen are here: jealousy (really envy), praise of an object without the disclaimer (in this case spitting), and unintentional calamity from bad eyes. Slovak peoples, however, add a causal factor: they believe that an evil eye is caused directly by one thing, letting an infant return to the breast after it has been weaned. Such a person will develop inordinate desires and will then have "bad eyes," eyes reminiscent of the *jettatore*, eyes that cause calamity. Slovak mothers therefore exert all their wills to see that this does not happen.

Stein goes on to argue that it is precisely this weaning process, exaggerated among Slovaks but by no means limited to them, that can predispose people to jealousy (the Slovaks consider themselves "the most jealous people in the world," a distinction I thought belonged to Italians), envy, and resultant belief in the evil eye. For according to Stein, the predisposition to evil-eye belief appears to be similar to that of witchcraft:

The common belief in witches tells us something about the mother's quite open ambivalence toward her children, and shows a predominantly orally oriented mechanism of defense, which splits the mother image into the good, devoted mother and the dangerous, treacherous witch . . . the belief in devouring demons is a projective manifestation of ideas which are clearly preoedipal and are very often connected with food sacrifices to deceased ancestors. This ritual is rather widespread and is an institutionalized attempt to undo oral-destructive fantasies against the retaliating mother elaborated by Melanie Klein.[14]

In other words, into the near-perfect world of nursing baby come the twin problems of teething (baby bites mother, mother reacts in pain and anger) and, sooner or later, weaning. The deprived baby responds in two ways: he builds fantasies of biting rage against the mother; and at the same time fears that the mother will retaliate by striking or even annihilating him for his rage. To be sure, the mother's real ambivalence toward the baby's endless demands on her help to fuel these fantasies. Then when the breast, the one thing the baby wants most, is in fact taken away in weaning, the situation is compounded by feelings of loss, separation, and abandonment. According to Melanie

Klein's model, the baby must resolve this painful dilemma and does it as follows: first, the mother image is split up into the "good mother" who has always fed on demand without any conditions and the "bad mother" who takes away nourishment and/or love arbitrarily and who corresponds to infantile fantasies of ogress, annihilating witch, and so on. Second, the baby also splits its own image into good and bad selves: a good baby who loves and is loved and a bad one who is endlessly desirous, envious, and ultimately destructive of that which he loves. "In this sense," Stein concludes, "the evil eye can be understood metaphorically as a spat-out introject, an externalized, repudiated 'bad self' and 'bad mother.' "[15] In other words, evil-eye belief allows a person to literally spit out the bad parts of his personality and say, "It is not I who envy; I would never do such a thing; there are evil-eyed ones out there who envy me."

The evil-eye system can thus be considered a cultural defense mechanism for handling the "return of the repressed." That is, a person's repressed "bad self–bad mother" manifests itself again and again in acceptable form—the envy and power of *other people's* bad eyes. And the power of those eyes to harm, even to destroy oxen, derives from the same infant fantasy level:

"Having wanted the breast caused it to go away, and destroyed (in fantasy) the mother. To want is to alienate the very object of one's desire."[16] Small wonder then that people from evil-eye cultures continually expect envious eyes to strike when they get something desirable.

An interesting footnote to this Slovak system is a belief that Frederick Elworthy records in his essay on evil eye. Many Hindus believe

that an invisible spirit is born with the child and that it is necessary for the mother to keep one breast tied up for forty days, feeding the child only with the other, by which means the spirit is starved to death. If the child is fed from both, it will grow up with the evil eye.[17]

Is this not the same belief, the same basic psychology, in an alternate form? I think it is. Worth recalling, too, is the special susceptibility to evil eye of cows and milk and butter. Milk as a connecting link among these images seems to be indicated.

That this connection may not be an idle one is suggested by a study by two anthropologists, Vivian Garrison and Conrad Arensberg.[18] After studying the research on evil eye, they conclude, in part, that what distinguishes evil-eye cultures is the presence of dairying/herding groups who compete for land and livelihood with settled farmers. Economies like this are typical of the so-called circum-Mediterranean zone, where the authors place the origin of the evil eye in Neolithic times (neither milk nor evil eye are prevalent in China). In this area have long been found complex societies in which a weak bureaucracy, as in Italy, tries to govern a mixed economy made up of settled peasant farmers and often-nomadic herders. The bureaucracies seldom administer fairly. The real strength therefore, is to be found in the institution of personal patronage. That is, these societies are dominated by strong men—sheiks, landlords, *padrones*, and other personal protectors—who actually maintain an orderly trade between their opposing peasant and peasant-nomad clienteles.

Now it is these patrons, or *padrones*, according to Garrison and Arensberg, who are significant in the typical evil-eye event. They describe this event as a symbolic restatement of the social structure. It includes a "gazer" (actual or suspected), a "gazee" (actual or one who fears he may be gazed upon), and the action of the gazee to protect some possession of his by displaying a sign of protection (the amulet such as a *corno*) symbolizing his patron. By means of this display of the amulet, the gazer or his gaze is thereby averted and the possession is safe. Or, if the possession suffers damage, the gazee moves to fix it through some supernatural cure such as the oil and water ritual. The important thing according to the authors is that when faced with a threat, the gazee merely displays the symbol of his patron, thus averting damage or loss.

The authors argue that this event is based on the everyday reality of the circum-Mediterranean zone. There, the threat of confiscation or destruction of a peasant's property (produce to the tax collector, boys to the janissaries, girls to the harems, anything of value to the ever-present raiders or corrupt officials) has long been and still is a constant fact of life. The people who live there expect to be taxed on the basis of their "apparent style of life." They are not only in constant danger of having their goods seized, they are also continually endangered by envious neighbors who can report on their wealth. Thus, *one does not display goods*. It is easy enough to see how in this situation, the role of the *padrone*, or powerful protector, was and is crucial. The peasant is protected not by the laws of a bureaucracy in which he has no faith, but by the threat of retaliation that his *padrone* can inflict on whoever tries to take what is his. The godfather in Mario Puzo's novel is just such a *padrone*. When the law fails his undertaker friend, the godfather alone has the power to administer the justice known as "talon justice"; and the story makes clear that had the undertaker accepted the god-father's care earlier, the threat of his retaliation would have strongly discouraged the original crime.

Understood in this way, the symbol of protection (the amulet) when raised against a gazer/confiscator carries this warning: "Beware, I am protected, and my *padrone* (or patron saint, or god) will retaliate if you harm me or mine." At the same time, the amulet functions as a call to the protector and/or his henchmen for help. Therefore, what distinguishes the evil-eye event from the witchcraft event it derives from according to Garrison and Arensberg is the presence of this third party. Where witchcraft is essentially a two-party transaction—one person casts a spell to which another reacts by retaliation with magic of his own—*mal occhio*, as befits its origin in more complex societies, is a more complex three-party event. The third party is the patron whose power can be invoked not by incantation but by the mere display of a symbol—a display that wards off harm by the threat of retaliation rather than its use.

If it were needed, a final proof of the patron's importance in feudal villages (and the Italian Mezzogiorno has retained the padronal structure to virtually the present day) can be found in the structure of punishment that Dante envisions in his *Inferno*. There, the lowest circle of hell is reserved for those who commit what must be the most heinous of sins: betrayal of their patron.

Silver amulet in the shape of a siren, Naples.

Neapolitan amulet with frog seated on crescent moon. Note again the blending of Christian and pagan imagery.

Chapter Three

*Seeing. We might say that the whole
of life lies in that verb—if not
ultimately, at least essentially. . . .
To see or to perish is the very
condition laid upon everything
that makes up the universe.*

de Chardin

*The animus is in the heavenly
heart . . . by day it lives in the eyes
(i.e. in consciousness).*

Jung

*In Morocco, it is said that Evil Eye
owns two-thirds of the burial
ground.*

Westermarck

It seems fair at this point to say that beneath the considerable variety of beliefs and rituals pertaining to evil eye,
some common structural dynamics can be
discerned, primarily envy, the institution
of personal patronage, and preoedipal anxieties of destruction and separation. From
the alchemical symbology of oil and water
comes the further suggestion that an earlier belief in soul loss underlies the *mal
occhio* complex; and this belief implies a
kind of separation (of soul from body) as
well. What now remains to be seen is the

extent to which these and other structures can explain the role of the eye in *mal occhio*. For in the final analysis we cannot avoid asking the broader question: "Why is it the eye, and precisely the eye, that so often comes up the nervous organ, the organ to which is attributed not so much a profound value (we can understand that) but this wide-ranging mistrust and malevolence as well?"

The tidiest answer, of course, would be some conclusive proof that discernible physical harm can emanate from the human eye.* But such proof is slow in coming and slower still in being acceptably demonstrated. Short of that, one must look to anthropological, psychological, and mythological evidence. In each direction the dynamics already enumerated reappear, a fact that argues for their centrality in vision. Most important for this discussion, the theme of separation anxiety is reflected in two major separations that will be used as focal points: one was posited by Sigmund Freud early in his career; the other is referred to again and again by Joseph Campbell in his history of mythology. Taken together, they add depth and scope to our understanding of *mal occhio* while shedding some light as well on the consistently anxious symbology of vision.

To begin with Freud. In *Civilization and*

*This possibility cannot be entirely foreclosed. Several recent parapsychological experiments seem to indicate that a tangible force may indeed project from the eye. In June 1973, for example, at the First International Conference on Psychotronics in Prague, a Czech engineer, Julius Krmssky, showed a film in which he was able to turn on a light bulb by focusing his eyes on a diode switch. Consciousness-explorer Christopher Hills claims to have performed a similar feat in 1963 and several times thereafter with physicists as witnesses. Soviet scientists add the claim that they

Its Discontents, the great analyst mentions the idea that there must have been some primal "organic repression" that paved the way to civilization and the massive repressions it depends on. Given Freud's preoccupations, this crucial development would have to involve sex; given ours, it would have to involve vision; and it involves both. Twice mentioned in this late text (it appeared first in an early letter to Freud's close friend Fliess), the notion is this: the adoption of an upright stance by early hominids meant that sight, not smell, would henceforth be the dominant sense. Here is how Freud put it:

can record images emanating from the eye on a special film emulsion sensitive to the ultraviolet-wave spectrum. The Soviet parapsychologist Victor Inyushin reports similar emanations coming from the eyes of both animals and humans, presumably evidence of the so-called eyebeam.

The organic periodicity of the sexual process has persisted, it is true, but its effect on psychical sexual excitation has rather been reversed. This change seems most likely to be connected with the diminution of olfactory stimuli by means of which the menstrual process [once] produced an effect on the male psyche. Their role was taken over by *visual excitations*, which, in contrast to the intermittent olfactory stimuli, were able to maintain a permanent effect. The taboo on menstruation is derived from this "organic repression," as a defence against a phase of development that has been surmounted. . . . The diminution of the olfactory stimuli seems itself to be a consequence of man's raising himself from the ground, of his assumption of an upright gait; this made his genitals, which were previously concealed, visible and in need of protection, and so provoked feelings of shame in him.

The fateful process of civilization would thus have set in with man's adoption of an erect posture.

From that point the chain of events would have proceeded through the devaluation of olfactory stimuli and the isolation of the menstrual period to the time when visual stimuli were paramount and the genitals became visible, and thence to the continuity of sexual excitation, the founding of the family and so to the threshold of human civilization.[19] [Emphasis mine.]

In other words, where hominids, like most other animals, were excited periodically to sexual activity by what they smelled, upright *Homo sapiens* was excited more or less continuously by what he saw. Now there is no doubt that what interested Freud in all this was the degradation of the sense of smell and the new shameful attitude toward the naked human body that ensued from it. It is here, in Freud's view, that humans initially began to repress the sexual function (and its connection to excreta) as somehow animalistic, erecting in its place all the sublimations that are known as civilization. For our purposes, however, it is the elevation and consolidation of the sense of sight that assumes paramount importance. For it can be further inferred that this momentous step, this stunning consolidation of *cupiditas* in the human eye, must have had as its corollary not only shame but also remorse—a sense of remorse over what was lost: the "innocent eye." By this is meant man's eye before he stood up (an event which, in the paradoxical language of myth, is called a "fall"), the prelapsarian eye which, like the eye of infancy and childhood, is

the eye that perceives out of the pure pleasure of exercising its natural function. . . . Some of this quality may be preserved in maturity and is essential in the artist; but how is it lost? What is the guilty eye? The poet who composed the third chapter of Genesis, in describing the temptation and fall of Adam and Eve, puts the following words into the mouth of the "subtil snake" as he tempts with the forbidden fruit: "For God doth know that in the day ye eat thereof, then *your eyes shall be opened*, and ye shall be as gods, knowing good and evil. And when Eve *saw* that the tree was good for food, and that it was *pleasant to the eyes*, and a tree to be desired to make one wise, she did eat the fruit and shared it with Adam. And *the eyes of them both were opened*, and they knew that they were naked. And they covered themselves with fig leaves and hid for shame."

So, it would seem, the price of wisdom, of the knowledge of good and evil, is the loss of the innocent eye. Looking is no longer enough in itself. Looking becomes a means to an end, a tool—we lose paradise and are left with a deep and abiding nostalgia.[20]

While Freud might not approve the conjunction, the Biblical description indicates that both he and the poet of Genesis were responding to one and the same thing. That is, there evidently exists in human consciousness a deeply felt conviction that a primal separation once took place, and the eye is its symbol or agent. Before this (the chronology of the "event" in question is endlessly debatable; what appears beyond doubt, given the universality of "fall" myths, is the reality of a felt gap between humans and all other living things), the creature that was to become man lived as one with the rest of creation. His chemical sexuality was in accord with that of the other animals, as was the periodic rhythm of his existence. One is tempted to think of this innocent period as the time prior to the "light" of consciousness,* when man saw or sensed phenomena in all their virgin splendor and did not yet regard himself or repress himself, there being nothing to repress. With upright stance and the enthronement of vision, however, an enormous series of steps is initiated, leading inevitably to uniqueness, that is to say, separation. The hands are freed and vision is codified, fostering calculation and action at a distance; the resultant power in the manipulation of objects, in the development of more sophisticated tools with which to hunt and survive, all lead over time to more complex and successful forms of organization. But the loss, ah, the loss is not small, nor easily forgotten. Gone is the vegetal paradise of the ape with its innocent immersion in multisensual nature. Gone home and the certitude of instinct. Upright man sees not only to procreate and

*Carl Jung was only the first of many to relate the fall to the advent of consciousness, symbolized by limited vision. More recently, Christopher Hills states: "The whole Adam and Eve allegory is an outline of the process by which the 'Tree of Knowledge,' the nervous system, tempts us to accept sensory knowledge as real when all it does is present comparisons. Comparative knowledge, being dualistic and not direct perception, was called knowledge of Good and Evil . . . the experience we call ordinary waking 'consciousness' is merely the imaginative formulation of concepts and does not effectively lead to reality at all."[21]

{66}

to fashion tools; he sees himself objectively as well, seeing that he sees and that others see him.

Yet lest it should be imagined that the prelapsarian world was all visual roses, at least one other fact should be mentioned. It has long been known that direct eye contact among primates is a threat-inducing situation. (Actually the same holds true for other species; stare hard at a dog and it will turn away or otherwise display submission.) In the already-cited essay by Garrison and Arensberg, there is an account of a photographer's experience while trying to photograph rhesus monkeys that bears on this fact. As predicted, the photographer's first approach to film his subjects ended in failure. The monkeys showed such aggressive threat behavior that he could not get near enough to shoot at all. The photographer found, however, that if he averted his eyes, the monkeys stopped their threats. He was also surprised to find that if he looked at the monkeys through the camera, there were no threats either. The authors conclude:

We can guess that the gaze, as an act of engagement of two animals in an interaction, is very deep in the ethogram of our species and that it is related to biological and psychological responses of dominance and submission, which are also universal in the ethogram of the species.[22]

This is only to say that even before the "fortunate fall" added unknown quanta to its domain, the eye emanated power.

To be sure, the entire evil-eye complex is testimony to this ancient power of the eye, and certain phrases emphasize this more than others. In discussing evil eye in Ireland, an informant recalled how her grandmother would berate younger women for walking their children too often in public. Insisting that the children be covered up, the older woman would say, "Sure, and don't the eyes of the people *eat* them?" A similar ocular power finds expression among the Amhara people of Ethiopia. There it is an outcast artisan class called *budas* who are believed to inflict evil eye. It is said that the *buda*, "by his very nature, must eat others" with his eyes.[23]

Now this is a much more active conception of vision than the one that photography once evoked as its analogue; that is, that eyes were passive receptors, cameras merely, recording in the screening room of the mind the phenomena that take place "out there." A concept of eating-eyes, on the other hand, accords rather more closely with current ideas of vision. Far from merely recording, eye and brain are now thought to impose their own version of order upon reality by reaching out to select from the billions of light forms impinging on the retina the significant ones, the ones that give shape and depth and size and position to the agglomerations we call objects. The human eye, in short, *creates* the world of objects according to some still-mysterious template. This idea leads to some classic philosophical conflicts—conflicts between appearance and reality, between the world our eyes create and the one that truly exists—that have been given greater validity by the discoveries of modern physics. We now know, for example, that what we see as solid matter is mostly empty space; that what appears to be empty space between objects is in fact mostly filled with vibratory extensions of those objects; that of the vast range of vibrations that make up the energy spectrum (and matter is only a concentrated bundle of energy that gives off vibrations), the human eye can see only a fraction. It is blind to x rays, radio waves, ultraviolet rays, gamma rays, neutrinos, and a host of other waves and particles too numerous to mention; but they are there, they are everywhere, "they" are in continual contact with "us."

It is not only that our eyes miss a tremendous range of vibrations, however; eyes and mind apparently *interfere* in a fundamental way with those vibrational waves that they do "see." That is, the waves reflected from the vibrational pattern that we call "object" impinge on our retinas all right, but they then go through a transformation in the mind or brain where they are actually "imaged"—a transformation that causes the resultant object to appear *outside* one's body when really it (its image) is inside, a transformation that locates an object at a certain place according to visual clues that may or may not be accurate. There are many optical illusions that confirm this interference of the mind in vision; some of the best of them have been suggested by Vasco Ronchi of the National Institute of Optics, Arcetri, Italy.[24]

To begin with, Ronchi suggests that what we think we see, objects, are really better characterized as "effigies." They are "psychic representations" built up in the mind as a result of the interaction between outside wave patterns, which Ronchi calls the "ethereal image" of the object, and wave patterns emanating from the mind itself. The resultant interference patterns, or representations, or effigies, work very well in most visual ranges and so usually seem perfectly accurate. But if, as suggested by Ronchi, we think of some long-distance images we take for granted, it is easy to see how completely wrong they, and we, can be. For example, the sun and the moon appear to us as disks in the sky. Classical optics informs us that our eyes and brain judge such size and distance the way they always do—according to the angle that such objects subtend on the retina. The problem is that the sun we "see" is the same size as the moon we "see." That is to say, our minds create a sun that is roughly the same size as the moon, even when we know this to be a false image. In the same way, the stars we "see" all appear to be and are judged to be about the same size and distance from us, even though we know some are near and relatively small while others are unimaginably large and distant. Finally, even though we know it is the same object we always see, the image of the moon we create at the horizon is far larger than the image we create of the same moon at zenith. In short, our eyes create "effigies." In short, our eyes are programmed to create the illusions of surface, of solidity, of size and distance, of boundaries between us and others, of a *projected reality* that evolution has judged to be critical to one limited range: our terrestrial survival.

That this is not the only reality, that it is in fact a veil between us and that *other reality* of which seers and mystics have always spoken, seems even clearer when we consider the case in light of the age-old metaphor of vision as reflection; wherein the created universe is likened to a mirror in which God (or the "I" of the self in the case of mere mortals) contemplates him/her/itself. From this viewpoint, the normal reality that our eyes see merely reflects what we, *Homo sapiens*, are. It is no more real than the entirely different universe which an ant's eye reflects to it, or a bird's eye to it, or a serpent's to it.

In truth, such a universe begins to seem depressingly solipsistic. At the same time, however, interesting visual implications derive from this notion of the universe as self-created reflection. Eyes then take central place at the core of our universe, the place from which it and we come and go. We are what we see; or mirrorlike, we see what we are. We believe what we see; or we see what we believe. From such a point of view, it is easy to understand the sense of the longstanding metaphor that eyes are "the seat of the soul." In Hebrew, for example, the pupil of the eye is called *ishon*, or little man; similarly, the German *Mannlein in Auge* and the Spanish *la niña del ojo* both refer to the essential person or soul embodied in the eye. It is equally easy to see how the tenuous nature of such a visual universe, shifting always, reflecting reflections of such doubtful substance, should give rise to a host of anxieties. The guilty eye in Genesis is but one prominent example. More to the point, Narcissus embodied the peril of reflection to the Greeks: he was thought to have fascinated himself (recall that "fascination" is another name for evil eye) by gazing too long at his own perfect likeness reflected in a pool.

That ideas of the soul and the problem of reflection are related is demonstrated more graphically in a lengthy discussion in Frazer's *Golden Bough*, a discussion that returns us to the problem of soul loss in *mal occhio*.[25] According to Frazer, it is commonly held among primitive peoples that reflection is dangerous primarily because the soul or shade is often believed to reside in just such a reflection. Thus, the Motumotu of New Guinea believed when they first saw their reflections in a mirror that they were seeing their souls. Likewise, to keep sorcerers away from the home, Aztecs would commonly leave a bowl of water with a knife in it behind the entrance door. Any sorcerer seeing his reflection (and thus his soul) pierced by a knife was sure to flee. Similarly, it is the custom among orthodox Jews to cover all mirrors in a house where someone has died. Were this not done, it is feared that a person's soul, projected out of his person in the shape of his reflection, might be carried off by the ghost of the departed one lurking about the house.

The suggestion offers itself that this same constellation of beliefs underlies certain evil-eye customs. The eye that "eats" must be considered, at least at times, to hunger for souls. Given that the soul is thought to be so loosely anchored to the body—particularly those most vulnerable souls of children, pregnant women, new brides, and all those in a weak or transitional state—one would expect that the precarious state would be much feared and guarded against. And so it is. In Mexico, for example, virtually all childhood diseases have traditionally been attributed to the work of evil eye (*mal ojo*). Accordingly, one old preventive measure consists of tying a red string around the wrist or ankle of vulnerable children. Ordinarily, this might seem a mysterious tactic. But if we look to Frazer again, we find a custom among the Lolos, an aboriginal tribe of China, that sounds almost identical. The Lolos feared that a person's soul (or one of his souls) could leave the body either in sleep, in sickness, via reflection, or through the agency of soul catchers. Therefore, when the Lolos considered that a missing soul had returned, they would "tie a red cord around the wrist of the sick man to 'tether his soul,' and this cord is worn until it withers and drops off.''[26] In much the same way, among the Kenyaks of Sarawak, a medicine man has been known to recall the stray soul of a child and fasten it firmly to its body by tying a string around the child's right wrist.

Such striking similarity argues that the Mexican custom as applied to *mal ojo* is a survival of a more primitive belief in and fear of soul loss as the cause of the sickness. And here it is interesting to note that once again ancient Greek conceptions of the soul give added substance to this interpretation. To begin with, it must be pointed out that the earliest Greeks, as Onians amply demonstrates,[27] had two distinct entities in mind when they referred to soul. The first was called ''thymos'' ($\Theta \upsilon \mu \acute{o} s$), the breath soul seated in the lungs and associated with blood, breath, thought, and speech. As the essence of waking consciousness, the thymos was dulled by sleep and wine and was shattered at death. The senses were thought to be manifestations of this soul—the eyes breathed a hot vapor or flame in vision, and ''to 'look at' in early Aeolic was to 'breathe at.' ''[28] Eyes were, in this sense, consciousness; in Latin this conscious soul was referred to as the ''animus.''

The second soul was known as the psyche ($\Psi \upsilon \chi \acute{\eta}$), in Latin referred to as the

The most common of amulets against *mal ojo* in Mexico is a seed called *ojo de venado*, "deer's eye" (*Thevetia nitida*). Its use underlies the link between seed and soul and eye.

"anima" or "genius." The psyche was "a second party distinct from and not reflecting the conscious self,"[29] which meant that it was akin to our unconscious. The seat of this second soul, or psyche, was variously in the head, the spinal column, the knees, and the thigh bone; it manifested in the body as fat or marrow (brain or bone marrow), hence its connection with olive oil. Its essence, however, was vapor, thereby being related to the body as vapor is to liquid, that is, heat could cause it to vaporize and presumably to depart. Maintained, indeed operative in sleep as dreams, the psyche survived the body at death to become the shadow soul that roamed about Hades. Perhaps its most important function was as the generative force in life; its connections with procreation, with seed and semen, with all the manifestations of male strength and sex such as beard, hair, horns (all growing from its main seat in the head) are many. Not surprisingly, this seed-soul was believed by the patriarchal Greeks to manifest preeminently in mature males but not in women or in boys prior to puberty.

One of the psyche's most important functions was as a binding force. It bound not only the body but also the universe. Anaximenes held that "just as our psyche being aer holds us together, so do breath (or *pneuma*) and aer encompass the whole world."[30] That is, as psyche was variously thought to surround the universe as a stream or river (*Okeanos*), so it was thought to bind the body and was its strength. When it was unloosed—in sleep or in love (which was said to unloose the knees) or in grief—the body was perceived to lose its strength and go slack. Consequent to these ideas, there was thought to be a gradual depletion of the liquid embodying this soul in all the instinctive drives it governed, such as procreation, rage of battle, and grief, until finally it was completely released in death; whatever was left was burned off or released in cremation. Clearly, this psyche, or binding force, was something to be maintained, revivified if possible, envied in those who appeared to possess it in abundance, regretted when lost.

Now if we consider that in all likelihood "the original amulet was the cord itself,"[31] as it was for the Lolos, the Kenyaks, and latterly the Mexicans, we can infer that *mal occhio* amulets, many hung about the neck even today, were in the primary sense also meant to be a binding force. Thus the simple string, bound about the wrist, was apparently meant to emulate the soul's binding force. In this way it could help ward off evil eye, which must have

Like the red cord of the Lolos, this wristband from Brazil is worn until it falls off, usually in about two months. The words printed on it— Lembranca do Senhor do Bon-fim da Bahia— invoke a patron saint of Bahia.

Syrian eye-charm for neck-lace, 3¾ inches high.

been viewed as an unbinding or loosening or perhaps vaporizing (analogous to the act of love) of the soul. The Roman custom of providing a child with a protecting "bubble," or *bulla*—a necklace containing a *fascinum* to ward off evil eye—until he reached puberty suggests the same thing: the amulet did the binding duty for the child's as yet immature psyche-soul. The olive oil and water ritual elucidated earlier (see page 45), wherein mixis indicates loss of tension in the binding force of the soul, would seem to reinforce this notion. Other Greek notions that connect with and reinforce this binding idea are the conceptions of the binding of fate as well as that of being bound in society by ties with family and neighbors. These bindings, too, are in jeopardy in the *mal occhio* event.

One problem that arises, of course, is that the notion of soul changed greatly over the centuries following its first mention by Homeric Greeks. In fact, by the fifth century B.C. the Greeks themselves were employing the words psyche and thymos interchangeably to refer to soul. This may help us to understand first of all how the eyes, originally associated with thymos-consciousness, become thereafter associated with soul in general. Secondly, it prepares us for the fact that the idea of soul seems eventually to be subsumed by the

*It is hard to know if later practices of conserving soul-stuff derive from this same merging of the two ideas, thymos and psyche. What is clear is that cults existed for whom conservation of generative stuff (semen) represented a way to achieve immortality. As Onians points out: "... this will explain why it was believed that Attis, being castrated, did not suffer death in the ordinary way: his body did not corrupt, his hair continued to grow, and his little finger to move, why also the Gospel to the Egyptians made the cessation of death dependent on the cessation of procreation ... and in the Fall the linking of death with sexual shame. The Gnostics did not castrate or abstain from intercourse but religiously avoided begetting of offspring and practised 'self-collection,' collection of psyche, whenever seed was emitted."[32]

idea of consciousness. Thus, as consciousness comes to mean more and more, as conscious control comes to identify man as opposed to the rest of creation (identified as instinct), it is the soul as consciousness that becomes the entity that survives (or wants to survive) after death. For unlike the original psyche that was more or less instinctual, thereby taking delight in both procreation and rage without thought of the consequences, the soul as consciousness or ego seeks to survive, seeks to conserve. Consciousness, that is, worries about the expending of generative stuff (the stuff of its immortality), fears that others want it, indeed fears that any manifestations of generative stuff elicit envy in others. Thus the world of *mal occhio*. Thus children, pregnant women, crops, cattle, manifestations all of abundant generative stuff or soul, are thereby subject to envy and attacks of *mal occhio*. *

Call it soul, or psyche, or ego, or consciousness, the point is that eyes have always had a great tendency to get associated with the animating spirit. And this hovering between illusory versions of reality has unquestionably made the eyes one of the body's weak links. *Mal occhio* aside, the range of ills that can strike the eyes is endless. They run from simple my-opia to hysterical blindness to jabbing out one's eyes to maintain one's purity. (Legend has it that Santa Lucia, the Italian patron saint of vision, tore out her eyes to discourage an overly aggressive suitor. He got the message and she kept her virginity; and so impressed was God by her devotion that He not only restored Lucia's vision, but granted her as well the power to cure eye diseases, *mal occhio* included.) Nor is it only hysterical saints who worry about their eyes. Recently, a Gallup poll indicated that more than any other medical problem, Americans fear loss of vision— not surprising in a culture whose addiction to visual stimulation, to those screens (television, film, computer printout) that screen it from reality, seems impervious to overdose. No doubt such worry causes its own problems. One eye doctor estimates that 75 percent of the people who consult eye doctors have neurosis as their major difficulty. Another maintains that physical problems of psychic origin are more frequent in the eye than in any other part of the anatomy.

But what is to be done? Since at least the time of the fall, vision has remained a very tenuous and impressionable entity. Having long since ceased to be natural or in-stinctive organs, eyes often become the target of the guilty mind. Oedipus is, of course, the type case: having committed the ultimate transgression, he blames his eyes, tears them out, and wanders blind ever after. Tiresias, too, saw what was forbidden (some say it was the naked goddess Athena, others that it was two snakes copulating). As punishment he was transformed into a woman for seven years, whereupon, as witness to both sides of reality, male and female, he was called upon by Zeus and Hera to judge whose was the greater joy in lovemaking. Tiresias agreed with Zeus that it was woman's, hence Hera struck him blind; without eyes, of course, he became a seer.* Still, both myths bear the same message: to see what is not to be seen is to risk blindness.

Actaeon was yet another mythic victim of seeing "beneath the veil." While out hunting, he happened to chance upon Artemis (or Diana) bathing naked in her forest pool. For his "oversight," he was immediately transformed by the goddess into a stag, thence to be slain by his own hounds, who knew him not. Others who see the great goddess naked, even in effigy, suffer the same fate. Tacitus in his Roman history writes of the Anglii (ancestors of the modern English) and their ritual bathing of the earth goddess's image. Slaves performed the bathing function, after which all were

*Tiresias, significantly, is the only shade met by Odysseus in Hades "whose senses stay unshaken within him." (*Odyssey,* X, 493.) We can guess that this thymos-immortality granted to him had something to do with his blindness and prior to that with his having been both male and female.

apparently considered so taboo that they were drowned in a lake. Tacitus ends his account delicately: "Thus mystery begets terror and a pious reluctance to ask what that sight can be which is allowed only to dying eyes." [33]

The sight allowed only to dying eyes. The Bible is rather more prosaic about it. In the Gospel of Matthew it is written:

I say unto you, that whosoever looketh on a woman to lust after her hath committed adultery with her already in his heart. And if thy right eye offend thee, pluck it out and cast it from thee. [34]

Which is, recall, just what Santa Lucia did. And which the psychological literature assures us not a few psychotics do. Other texts carry more specific prohibitions. The sixteenth-century Arabian tale "The Perfumed Garden," carries a warning that looking into the cavity of the vagina is injurious to the eye. The Bushmen of South Africa have at it from the opposite tack. They believe that the glance of a menstruating girl's eye may fix a man in position and change him into a tree. And here it is impossible not to hear echoes of the Medusa legend, whereby one glance from that snake-framed visage could turn a man to stone. (The gorgoneum, incidentally, is used extensively in Italy as a doorknocker to ward off evil eye.)

What seems obvious in all this, the com-

mon thread running from Freud through
the Bible to the Medusa, is that everywhere are encountered taboos, symbolic
or otherwise, that bear the same message:
There are things that are not to be seen
with the naked eye, the discriminating
eye, the guilty eye, the eye that by its
very nature is reductive. For the eye always and everywhere reduces what is
manifold and incomprehensible to what is
manageable and useful and desirable. Just
as the taboos themselves to an orthodox
Freudian reduce to simple sexual repressions. But are we to believe the matter is
all that simple, that the sight permitted
only to dying eyes can be reduced to infantile sexuality after all? Are we not re-

minded always that the price for such re-
ductions is ignorance?

Still, there is no doubt that sexuality is
involved. There is no doubt that desire,
cupiditas, is involved. There is no doubt
that the female form, the mother, and
union are involved. And that vision as it
encounters and expresses all these things
is involved and in a way that regards itself
as both shameful and necessary, sinful and
transcendent, traducer as well as initiator
to the highest good of which humans are
capable; for the eye, it must be remembered,
was the agent of the fortunate fall. In sum,
we can guess that what incites fear and
thereby taboo cannot be alone the sight of
the naked female form, maternal or not,
divine or not, *in flagrante delicto* or not,
but something more, some immense problem or mystery it represents. It must be
something that, lens size notwithstanding, cannot be reduced to externals, to the
basic visual elements of light and shadow,
figure and ground (a brief look at any por-
nographic film will demonstrate that). It
must be something that cannot be looked
at from a safe distance for there is none:
discrimination itself (that is, distance itself) must be scuttled. It must be something that has to do not only with sex and
desire but with the very source of those
things, with the essential process of which

they are but symbols like both maternity and *mal occhio*, the uncovering of which— but how? and at what cost?—leads to true knowledge, that is, self-knowledge.*

In symbolic terms, therefore, those who see too far — Milton, Galileo — go blind. Those who wish to see far, to be seers like Tiresias, must go blind. Jews make no images of Jahweh; he is the all-seeing who is not to be seen. In Zen meditation, the eyes are kept open but unfocused. *Reality*, the reality beneath the veil, is too powerful, too all-encompassing, too self-consuming for normal vision. And here, as it will again and again, the imagery circles back once more to the veil. It is the veil met by Oedipus, by Actaeon, by Tiresias. It is the veil of taboo, the veil shrouding the oldest mystery, the primary deity, the primeval female whose proudest words remain: "No one has lifted my veil."

Chapter Four

*I am she that is the natural
mother of all things . . . my name,
my divinity is adored throughout
the world, in diverse manners, in
variable customs, and by many
names . . . the Phrygians that are
the first of all men call me the
Mother of the gods of Pessinus; the
Athenians, which are sprung from
their own soil, Cecropian Minerva;
the Cyprians, which are girt about
by the sea, Paphian Venus; the
Cretans, which bear arrows,
Dictynian Diana; the Sicilians,
which speak three tongues, in-
fernal Proserpine; the Eleusinians,
their ancient goddess Ceres; some
Juno, others Bellona, others He-
cate, others Ramnusie . . .; and the
Egyptians, which are excellent in
all kind of ancient doctrine, and by
their proper ceremonies accus-
tomed to worship me, do call me by
my true name, Queen Isis.*

Apuleius

The mother goddess. So many are her
manifestations and so various her
consorts and sons and lovers that one hardly knows which ones to mention. It should

The Roman
Diana of Ephesus
retained the same
qualities as her
original, the
Greek goddess
Artemis: virgin
mother, multi-
breasted nurtur-
er, familiar of
animals.

perhaps be noted first that in Mesopotamia she was, in her earliest manifestations, most often connected with cattle and dairying:

The earliest known temple compounds in the history of civilization arose in this area ca. 4000 B.C. and by their form suggested a reference to the female genitalia, specifically the matrix of the cosmic mother goddess, Cow. The milk of the sacred cattle raised within their enclosures was equivalent to that of the mother goddess herself, whose calf was the animal of sacrifice.[36]

When one takes account of the fact that in Egypt there was another cow-goddess manifestation, named Hathor, who was the original of Isis, the mother goddess; that in Rome, Isis's counterpart was Diana of Ephesus, the special protectress of domestic cattle; and that many amulets *contra mal occhio* take forms sacred to Diana—silver being her metal, the crescent moon being her sign—one is reminded of the connective link between dairying and *mal occhio*, and thence between the mother goddess and *mal occhio*. The connection is reinforced when one looks at her consorts, the first of which must be the bull. This is the mythic lunar bull whose most well known manifestation is the Minotaur in Crete. His bull horns, shaped like the crescent moon, have been associated with the mother goddess for millennia.

Earlier the mother goddess had for her consort a serpent, the same serpent which sloughs lives like skins and turns ever in its circle of eternal return, never dying but getting absolutely nowhere. The serpent consort, too, suggests a link to *mal occhio*, most notably through Mercurius, the alchemist's soul symbol whose nature was oil and water. For the Titans, that order of divine beings who were supplanted by Zeus and his Olympians, were sometimes imaged as half-serpent, half-human creatures. Since Mercurius, or Hermes, had a direct connection to the Titans (Greek sources say that his mother, Maia, was a nymph or Titaness; Roman cosmology makes him the son of Saturn, the Roman counterpart of the Titan Cronus), and since his symbol, the caduceus, bespeaks even more obviously his connection to serpents, the associations of Mercurius, and thereby *mal occhio*, with the mother goddess take on added substance.

Bull and serpent are merely the most conspicuous of the figures associated with the goddess, however. Besides these, there are lion consorts and birds of prey; double sons and double husbands; and sometimes the goddess herself is doubled—as in Mesopotamia to become Inanna, queen of heaven, and Ereshkigal, queen of hell; or in Greece, to become Aphrodite, goddess of

Mercury bronze, Dutch-Florentine, c. 1603. Mercury's caduceus was said to ward off the eye of Juno made envious by his errands for rival gods.

love, and Persephone, goddess of death; or in the Eleusinian mysteries to become Demeter, goddess of earth and grain, and Proserpine, goddess of the underworld. And always with her is the son-lover, Dumuzi or Adonis or Attis or Osiris or Dionysus, the dying and reborn god who dwells with one aspect of the goddess in life and with the other in death.

In truth, the cast of characters that has multiplied and been transformed into countless mythologies over thousands of years is often difficult to keep straight. Yet a single idea emerges always. It is that the mother goddess or great mother symbolizes the eternal paradox of existence: matter quickens into life and decays into death, each feeding on the other endlessly. The earth gives birth to creatures without end and consumes them almost as fast as they are born. And while we are used to dualistic thinking that tries to separate these two functions, the fact is that in the earliest manifestations of this deity the two were not separate but one: the one goddess whose son-lover always dies, but who always rises again reborn. Nowhere is she more graphically embodied than as the black goddess Kali of India (it is worth noting that in southern Italy there are many places where a major object of worship is the Black Madonna—Mary, mother of Jesus, in her aboriginal, mother-goddess aspect), who with her right hand gives and in her left holds a raised sword, Kali who gives birth to all beings of the universe, yet whose tongue lolls long to lick up their living blood. She wears a necklace of skulls; her kilt is of severed arms and legs. She is, in the words of Joseph Campbell:

Black Time, both the life and death of all beings, the womb and the tomb of the world; the primal, one and only, ultimate reality of nature, of whom the gods themselves are but the functioning agents.[37]

Now what took place at the beginning of the Neolithic Age were just those discoveries that gave this image life. The chief of these must have been the terrific impact that resulted when men, or more likely women, saw that burying a seed in the ground brought forth a new plant exactly like the one from which it came. This meant that not only did living things die and come to life eternally, but more, that they were connected; that death *was* life; that burial *was* rebirth; that the killing of plants when harvesting them was only temporary and led after burial of the seed to new plants; and that what was needed to ensure the fertility of plants and animals and humans was death and sacrifice, that in truth, death and sacrifice *were* fertility.

We now, of course, know these things to be scientifically true: dead matter does indeed fertilize the soil; reproduction without death would in fact be a monstrosity. But in the earliest planter villages such notions were presumably sensed by homologues—the waxing-waning moon, the rising-setting sun, the burial and growth of seed, the rising and falling of the phallus in sex. The understanding and accord with such mysteries were demonstrated by the enactment of ritual, one of which suffices to illustrate the type. It is a rite of the Marind-Anim, headhunting cannibals of Dutch South New Guinea, and it was first recorded by ethnologist Paul Wirz. Performed to reenact the world-beginning action of their gods known as the Dema, the ceremony goes on for several days and is very complex. Its most telling moment, however, occurs at the conclusion of the boys' puberty rites—a drama that is led up to by a sexual orgy during which everyone in the village except the initiates is allowed to copulate freely amid a crescendo of chants, drums, and bullroarers. Then on the final night

a fine young girl, painted, oiled, and ceremonially costumed, is led into the dancing ground and made to lie beneath a platform of very heavy logs. With her, in open view of the festival, the initiates now cohabit, one after the other; and while the youth chosen to be last is embracing her, the supports of the logs above are jerked away and the platform drops, to a prodigious boom of drums. A hideous howl goes up, and the dead girl and boy are dragged from the logs, cut up, roasted, and eaten.[38]

The point—one is tempted to call it a "dying fall"—could hardly sear the mind more indelibly: that all is unity, that the world is sustained by death no less than life, that sex and death are one and the same and in divine embrace with food and fertility as well.

In the area we have been discussing, the Neolithic Near East, these themes or imprints were given shape by a single image: the mother goddess. In her could be expressed the complete cycle. She was the goddess of fertility, not only of crops and cattle but of men; she was simultaneously the goddess of death and rebirth. Transformed in innumerable ways throughout history, split up and separated into virgins and whores, mothers and witches, she was originally one, she was originally all.

Were these associations and attributes of the mother goddess the nub of the matter, they would yet be of interest to a discussion of evil eye, not least because they allow mention of the Medusa, that most famous of the negative or chthonic aspects of

Medusa head on North Italian coin, late 15th or early 16th century.

Gorgoneum painted inside Attic black-figure eye-cup, c. 6th century B.C. With apotropaic eyes on the outside of the cup as well, protection was thus doubled.

the mother goddess. Known primarily for her potent glance that could turn humans to stone, she also embodied lesser-known healing powers: Asclepius, the Greek god of healing, used the slain Medusa's blood to bring patients back to life. This healing aspect makes doubly sensible the use of the gorgoneum to ward off *mal occhio*. There is another and perhaps more critical connection to be noted, however. In 1937 M. E. L. Mallowan led an excavation in the Khabur Valley near the Euphrates River in Syria, at a place called Tell Brak. There Mallowan found a temple which he called the Eye Temple. It derives from a period of Mesopotamian settlement called the Jemdet Nasr period, dated somewhere between 3400 and 3000 B.C. The date makes it roughly contemporary with the very early cities of Sumer, located to the south and west. Figurines, vases, cylinder seals, and beads of all kinds are listed in Mallowan's catalogue of the Eye Temple. But most pertinent are the so-called eye-idol figurines of alabaster and terra cotta. Over three hundred intact specimens were found, the survivors of a store of fragments that must originally have numbered twenty thousand. Most have a flat, oblong body, tapering into an elongated neck and topped by the exaggerated, staring eyes. Originally, the eyes bore even more emphasis because

Eyes on a Su-
merian seal-
impression, 3rd
millennium B.C.
Eye-idols from
Tell Brak, c. 4th
millennium B.C.,
the drawings
after Mallowan.

Eyebrow designs
from contempo-
rary Morocco.
Note the similar-
ity between the
imagery of the
Brak eyebrows
and the Moroc-
can designs.

they were infilled with color, some faint traces of which remain.

Since this is the only place that such eye-idols have been found, they represent a bit of a puzzle. Mallowan reasoned that they were "benevolent and protective eyes, intended to bring good fortune to those who deposited and dedicated them to the presiding god or goddess of the temple."[39] Along with others, Mallowan concluded that this presiding deity must have been a form of the mother goddess. Known elsewhere in Mesopotamia as Ishtar or Inanna, her character and domain were similar to those we have seen: in Sumer her son-lover was called Dumuzi—perhaps the smaller figure included in some of the eye-idols. The only problem is that one finds at Tell Brak none of the usual aspects of motherhood so clear on goddess figurines from surrounding areas, that is, the prominent breasts, exaggerated belly and hips, and emphatic vulvae used to symbolize this deity from the Paleolithic onward. Indeed, where many of the earliest goddess figurines have minimal heads that are most often sightless, thus giving greatest emphasis to sitting or motionless lower torsos, these in Tell Brak are just the opposite: the staring, over-sized, and multiple eyes have become the focus of attention. Mallowan concluded that this difference represents nothing

{96}

more fundamental than a change to a more abstract iconography, and lets the matter rest. One must wonder, however.

For if Mallowan is correct that the eye-idols represent Ishtar—the stone rosettes found at Tell Brak were everywhere her sign—then we are here dealing with the same goddess as always; the one beneath whose veil lies the great mystery, of which even a brief glance demands its terrible price, blindness or even death. Only here, suddenly, her eyes take precedence over all more obvious female attributes to become her most prominent trait, to become indeed the very symbol of godhood. Surely the symbolism has significance beyond that of simple abstraction, which in any case is not so simple.*

Agreeing that it may be impossible to determine with precision the significance of developments that took place five thousand and more years ago, one can yet look to both internal and external evidence and draw some tentative conclusions. To begin with, the change itself—from an older motionless, sightless deity to one who sees—draws our attention to the fact that the values implicit in each type are opposed. A sightless, corpulent deity evokes ideas of permanence and stability, of a static, circular worldview, that is, such as settled agriculturalists might hold. A deity for

The stone rosettes from the Eye Temple at Brak have their modern descendants in this rosette amulet from Morocco.

*Erich Neumann in his book, *The Great Mother*, points out that the move to abstraction signifies, among other things, a turning away from the real world in favor of a more incorporeal, hence spiritual, view that is often

associated with cults of the dead. The change to abstracted eyes, therefore, implies a move away from the more obviously naturalistic attributes of female flesh emblematic of fertility, and toward the more spiritual attributes of eyes and the afterlife.

whom eyes and eyesight are primary suggests, on the contrary, a more mobile, active worldview in which open space and keen eyesight dominate—in a word, the world of the hunter-nomads. Now it is clear that in the Near East at the time of Tell Brak—as well as throughout the Mediterranean in both earlier and later millennia—the opposition and mixing of these two groups was an important fact of social and political life. For into the settled agricultural communities of the Levant, many of which were marked by mother-goddess worship, there continually infused the nomadic pastoralists of the surrounding foothills. With them the latter could always be expected to bring their generally more patriarchal, warlike values. When we find a deity such as the one at Tell Brak, then, in whom eyes are raised to prominence, in whom godhood has shifted from its usual locus in female fat to eyes and vision, we may well regard it as a product of some such infusion. And this suggests that a corresponding shift was taking place in the secular arena—a shift detrimental to the agriculturalists, for whom corpulent female flesh symbolized a circular way of life based on farming rhythms, and in favor of pastoralists for whom keen eyesight and movement were primary. It suggests that the more patriarchal worldview held by the nomads was gaining ground. In such a worldview, power—and for power read "generative force"—would be associated with the head, eyes and vision, rather than with female fat. Indeed, this is essentially what developed at a later time—notably among the Greeks and Hebrews of the first and second millennia B.C.—and to a more radical degree. Greek mythology, that is, conceives of generation as a male, cerebral prerogative: Zeus gives birth to Athena through his head; the psyche-soul resides in the brain marrow of mature males. At Tell Brak, to be sure, this displacement upward —the movement of godhood from female fat to female eyes—stopped well short of the complete shift to male gods it took among the Greeks. The pastoralists and their warrior kings and patriarchal gods have not assumed total control. Not yet.*

Aside from the above considerations, one still has at Tell Brak the idols, wherein the mother goddess is virtually reduced to those eyes. What of that, of the eyes themselves? Can we assume that, as it appears on the face of it, the worshipers at the Eye Temple suddenly found that all the old attributes of the mother goddess as fertility and death, womb and tomb could be more perfectly expressed in the symbol of those flat, staring eyes? Perhaps not suddenly.

*That they do, and with what consequences, can be seen on page 119.

{99}

The eyes on this face-pot from Tell Hassuna in north Iraq likewise suggest cowrie shells.

Perhaps it was a throwback to earlier iconography as at Jericho (about 7000 B.C.), where human skulls were clayed over and the eyes emphasized by cowrie shells— cowrie shells that Westermarck tells us were, even in twentieth-century Morocco, used as amulets against evil eye.[40] Perhaps it was in response to growing tensions between competing ideologies. But whatever the reasons and however long the preliminaries, it looks as if eyes at Brak somehow came to mean everything: both a path and a barrier, both an invitation and a warning, both love and threat, as in fact the goddess could be both loving:

The living creatures, the multitudinous people, bend
    the knee before her,
The "called ones" of the matriarchs, for the Queen,
Prepare immense quantities of food and drink,
The Lady refreshes herself in the land,
There is festive play in the land,
The young man soothes the heart of his spouse.
My Lady looks on in wonder from heaven's midst,
They parade before the holy Inanna.

and threatening:

My Queen, you are all-devouring in your power,
You kept on attacking like the attacking storm,
Kept on blowing louder than the howling storm,
Kept on moaning louder than the evil winds,
Your feet grow not weary,
You caused wailing to resound on the harp of lament.
My Queen, the Anunna, the great gods,
Fled before you like fluttering bats,
Could not stand before your awesome face.[41]

Spiral eyes
guarding the en-
trance to the an-
cient temple of
Hal Tarxien on
the island of
Malta.

Eyes on Spanish
pots, bones, and
stones from Los
Castellones, Al-
mizaraque, Prov-
enance, and Los
Millares, mid-2nd
millennium B.C.
Bronze-Age
plaques carved in
slatey stone from
Portugal and
Spain.

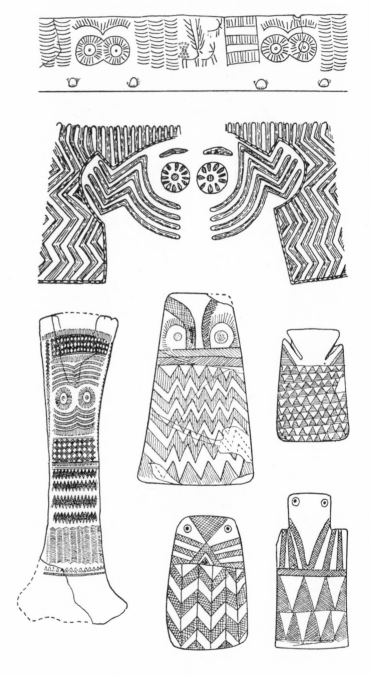

Indeed, the paired eyes of the goddess may well have come finally to represent a kind of stasis or balance, a symbol reconciling all the opposing powers—of love and threat, of generation and decay, of womb and tomb, of herder and farmer—the mystery of which human eyes can only mimic and should never presume to penetrate. Nor would such a unifying symbolism be all that apparent were the remains at the Eye Temple—both eye-idols and the many rosettes and eye carvings around the temple walls—the only evidence. Not even adding the roughly contemporary Horus eye symbology of Egypt would truly firm the case.

But if we look to the materials assembled by O. G. S. Crawford[42] and note the appearances of what he calls the "eye goddess" around the Mediterranean, in Spain and France, in Britain and Ireland, we come across some variations and further abstractions of eye symbolism which suggest that the Tell Brak development was considerably more than a local phenomenon. Consider, for example, the ancient temple at Hal Tarxien on the island of Malta. There the mother goddess's image is abstracted to an even more radical degree, such that only eyes are represented, and they are two huge spirals. Now this spiral motif in ancient cultures is so widespread that it

The *udjat eye,* or Horus eye, was a most common amulet in ancient Egypt. Lost in battle with the god Set, the left eye of Horus was restored by Thoth, and became the symbol for health, vigor, and rebirth.

*Recent carbon
dating has now
led to theories
that the mega-
lithic spirals of
Western Europe
are older than
the supposedly
parent ones in
the Near East. If
so, the spirals in
both places would
represent not
diffusion from
one to the other
but a case of par-
allel develop-
ment, or what
seems more
likely, descent
from an older,
common source
in the Paleolithic.
Further, we may
here again have
an instance of fu-
sion: the single
spiral one often
finds in Britain
may be, as is often
suggested, a solar
symbol of most
significance to
herder-nomads,
while the double
spiral (eyes) may
represent the mix
suggested above
—a balance be-
tween nomads
and town dwell-
ers, between
herders and
farmers. The re-
lationship be-
tween two other
symbols—the
single and double
axe—strikes one
as similar. Single
axes found on
such megaliths as
Stonehenge were

would take a much longer discussion than this to trace it fully. For our purposes it is sufficient to attend to only a few examples, first noting that Mallowan mentions, without illustration, the presence of spirals at Tell Brak. Far more well known are the spiral labyrinths of Crete, at the center of which lurked the Minotaur. Symbolically, this spiral labyrinth maps the path to the zone of death and rebirth but in a confusing, and thereby defensive, way; it can be penetrated only on condition of fulfilling its terms. Indeed, all labyrinths and mazes are said to suggest the same idea: the guarded entrance to a very privileged and dangerous zone. Noteworthy, too, is the spiral from Val Camonica in Italy, containing at its center not a bull but a pair of eyes. Beyond these are numerous spirals in tombs and guarding tombs—the eyes of the goddess often have this guarding function—from Sicily to Ireland, all of which suggest to Crawford the diffusion of the eye-goddess cult throughout pre-Roman Europe.*

The point to be made here has to do not so much with diffusion, however, as with the apparent fact that eyes and spirals at some point in the Neolithic period seem to have become interchangeable when symbolizing the mother goddess. This leads to a rather more expanded set of inferences. First, eyes that are also spirals suggest not

apparently both weapon and symbol to the male warrior caste of herders dominant there, representative "of its separateness and power. The process by which they were made was magical, and, since fire-forged, related to the sun."[43] Interestingly, the single axe appears later as an amulet *contra mal occhio*. In Minoan Crete and elsewhere in the Near East, contrarily, the double axe was a symbol associated with the mother goddess, her sacred bull, and fertility.

Multiple carvings on Kerbstone 52, northwest side of the mound, Newgrange, Ireland, Neolithic. Spiral stone guarding the entrance to the passage grave at Newgrange.

Double spiral and feet (or hands) carved on a stone from the Calderstones passage grave near Liverpool, Neolithic. Eye carvings on a stone from the passage grave at Knockmany, Ireland, Neolithic. Multiple arcs from stone carvings in the passage grave on Gavr Inis, Brittany, Neolithic. Stone goddess from St.-Sernin, southern France, perhaps late Neolithic.

only focus but its opposite—a spinning, whirling confusion of the visual field. There is thus the implication that vision in such a zone will be first subjected to scattering, will be whirled into a vortex to be unwound, deranged, and derationalized before becoming clear. The seer, that is, must go blind. In this sense, the eye spiral as symbol functions as a type for all other symbols: mistaken as the purveyors of the only reality, eyes and vision are at once signposts to knowledge and barriers to its achievement.* Concurrently, the two eyes of the goddess as spirals do have the potential to express that balance: a balance of two interconnected spirals or vortices (the spiral may be seen as a two-dimensional representation of the three-dimensional vortex or cone, which itself expresses one of the most fundamental patterns of nature) moving in opposing directions. These opposing spirals are, to be sure, multidimensional; their full meaning, like that of the goddess herself, can never be quite exhausted. But in part, at least, one eye must represent the spiral of generation moving outwards to yield birth, the other, the spiral of decay moving inwards to yield death; the one creating, the other consuming; one eye, recall, giving birth to the world of forms, the other destroying it in cataclysm and death. Nor is the son-lover

*Jung points out that this blockage of the "numinous" by symbols and myths that take on a primary life of their own "protects a person from a direct experience of god," for which few are prepared; it may, therefore, act as a safety valve to keep the unwary from stumbling, like Actaeon, upon Artemis naked in her pool.

The English monument Stonehenge, whatever else it may have been, was more than likely a device for predicting solar eclipses. The eclipse, a meeting of the sun and the moon, has long evoked in human thought the idea of a sacred marriage or divine connubium: the son, or sun, returns to the great mother, or moon. It is a symbol of balance or reintegration. A look at the plan of Stonehenge III, now dated about 2000 B.C., reveals the figure of a large sarsen circle of thirty stones, within which is a smaller horseshoe shape, or horn, or broken circle. If we take this plan to be the expression of the divine connubium (as its function is to predict the eclipse), it could be interpreted as the horn of the son or sun, returned to and enclosed by the complete circle of the mother. In other words, the shape of Stonehenge can be viewed as a balance symbol,

omitted from this spiral constellation. For if we think of one eye personified as the consuming, inwardly spiraling vortex of the mother, the symbol of implosion and gravity, the consuming eye that perennially attracts the son-lover to her in the "dying fall"; then conversely, we may think of the other eye as the exploding, outwardly spiraling vortex of the son-sun, the externally reborn god who rises after each death, the ever-exploding seed of life.

These spiral eyes of the goddess then do encompass a totality in the same way that

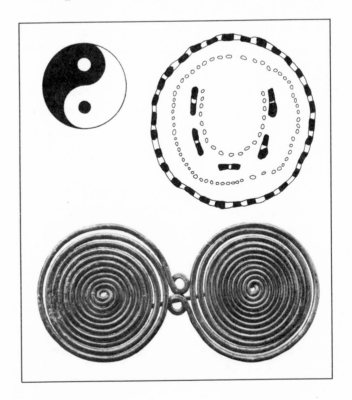

their apotropaic function encompasses the totality of existence: they guard both the womb-earth where life begins (as seed), and the womb-tomb where life ends—to begin, it is hoped, another life; the casket as seed impregnates the tomb as womb to yield the soul. Entry to either of these birthing points is through the labyrinth and possible only under the special conditions expressed by the spiral eyes themselves—a whirling, implosive obliteration of all distinction. And the identity between the two points is further emphasized by the fact that both are given voice through the same feminine deity: the maternal body is the focal point where spirit and matter meet, where spirit incarnates; the maternal earth is the tomb where they separate. Both must be guarded by spiral eyes because both are danger points, susceptible to contamination or seizure. But from what?

The logic of homeopathic magic leads one to suspect that the contamination would derive from other eyes. The power attributed to eyes, as well as ancient funerary practices, suggests the same thing. For example, the Etruscans placed the ashes of their cremated dead in funerary urns guarded by horns—the sign of the mother goddess and her son. In the late days of the Roman empire, the cremation practice was

in the same way that yin-yang is a balance symbol, in the same way that two interconnected spirals, suggesting two eyes, are a balance symbol. All symbolize the same constellations of death and life, sun and moon, masculine and feminine, son and mother, the divine connubium or reunion of opposites after a long separation.

revived, and urns have been found with the horned head as guardian. These symbols are said to have "guarded against a ghostly evil eye."[44] Protection from other eyes, then, has long been deemed necessary —protection of the soul from the eyes of hungry spirits seeking revenge. The revenge of the slain. That story is, in large part, the hunter's story.

Chapter Five

*It has been suggested that the daily
task and serious concern (of the
hunter) of dealing death, spilling
blood, in order to live, created a
situation of anxiety that had to be
resolved, on the one hand by a
system of defenses against revenge,
and on the other by a diminishment
of the importance of death.*

Campbell

Compared to the Neolithic period, the finds and facts about the Paleolithic Age of the hunt—an enormously long period in human history—are few and scattered. Much information, to be sure, has been derived from hunting groups in the Americas and Siberia, cultures which are presumed to have maintained intact a Stone-Age way of life for many thousands of years. This is not fully proven or provable, however, and one can therefore only draw some analogies with these modern hunters, and point out some few archeological finds that seem relevant to this discussion.

To begin with, it appears that in the imagination of the Stone-Age hunter, the eye was inextricably bound up with the act of killing. The "slaying eye" searches

In *Pilgrim at Tinker Creek*, Annie Dillard cites these words of an Eskimo shaman: "Life's greatest danger lies in the fact that men's food consists entirely of souls."

{ 111 }

out prey, fixes that prey in fear (as, for instance, the serpent is said to do) and ultimately kills. By analogy, the sun becomes the prototypical slaying eye. It rises each morning to obliterate the stars and moon that live at night. Each night, in turn, the slain stars and moon reappear in a starry miracle of rebirth. The analogy gives voice to the hope that the animal victims of the hunter's eye will likewise continually reappear, that food, in other words, will eternally be generated.

To insure this return of the slain, human groups for eons have performed all manner of ritual and magic and sacrifice. One of the oldest testaments to this appears in a Paleolithic cave at Drachenloch in the Alps. Dated as far back as 75,000 B.C., the cave contained bear skulls that it is clear were ritually buried.[45] For our purposes the interesting fact about the burial of this earliest of animal gods is the attention given to the eyes: the bear's own long bones were shoved through its eye sockets. Evidence gained from the Ainu people of Japan, who until recently performed similar bear rituals, indicates that those who make such sacrifices hope and pray for the animal's return. Yet the placing of the long bones implies something more, some underlying nervousness about the victim's visual memory. A reasonable conclusion is that regardless of the motives behind the animal sacrifice, the placing of the long bones was done to block out the old avenues of sight and thus forestall the possible blood revenge by the slain bear's spirit.

For the hunter's attitude toward eyes was, and is, clearly one of fear. The spirit or soul of the victim has seen the killer and may take revenge, either by capturing the living hunter's spirit or by displacing it and taking over the hunter's body. The spirit that is feared, apparently, is the "unhoused" soul or shade, that is, one without a body. Primitive people are said to believe that the embodied person is the optimum state of existence, and that the danger from an unhappy or vengeful ghost derives from the fact that it seeks to regain its former mode of embodiment. Conversely, eyes are often said to draw a person's or object's shadow soul toward them, according to which reasoning the soul is believed drawn to the camera's "eye" when it "takes" a photograph. Thus, dead eyes are feared as yet retaining this drawing power and are often covered and weighted down. Either way, the vengeful eyes are feared. And it is always the frontal, staring eyes of the killers—stereoscopic eyes—that are most potent. The sorcerer on the walls of the Paleolithic cave known as Trois Frères in France stares straight ahead at the viewer, as if demonstrating some unique visual power. The great carnivores all have frontal eyes, a feature separating them from most other animals, whose eyes are to the side. Such predatory eyes appear not to forget or forgive, as human eyes do not, and this idea survives in modern Morocco. There, when a man-eating panther is killed, the hunter, his own eyes closed, must immediately creep up on the dead animal from behind and attempt to blindfold the panther as quickly as possible. This to avert the danger of evil eye.*

One other find from the Paleolithic deserves mention. At a cave in Mal'ta near Lake Baikal in Russia was found the skeleton of a four-year-old child lying in fetal posture, facing east. With him were twenty figurines carved from mammoth ivory —the mother goddess in one of her earliest manifestations. Other objects in this cave included a plaque with a spiral design on one side and three serpents on the other, another spiral stippled on the side of an ivory fish, and a number of ivory birds. The spirals are the earliest examples of the art ever found.

What this constellation of objects means is not really known. But the serpent of eternal life associated with the labyrinth or spiral of death, the birds that normally symbolize the soul in flight, and the god-

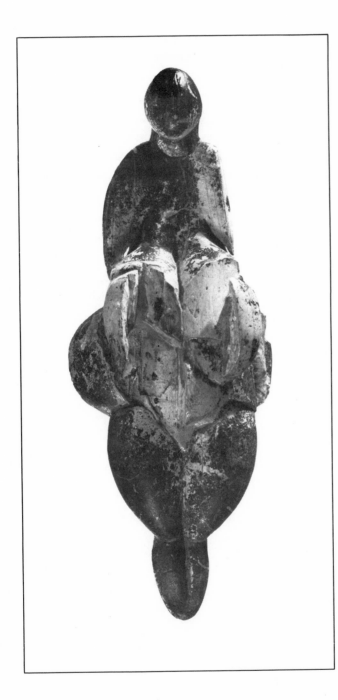

These Venus carvings are said to be the first objects of worship of *Homo sapiens*. They are associated with the mammoth-hunters of the Aurignacian period, a period that differed from the later bison-hunting period in its more settled nature and more female-oriented iconography. It is assumed that where bison-hunters had to be more nomadic to follow the herds, the mammoth-hunters were able to erect more permanent hunting stations (one mammoth kill could probably feed a group for a fairly long time). Thus, where nomadism would stress the male virtues of strength and speed of movement, resulting in a more patriarchal culture, this more settled way of life of the mammoth-hunters would seem to favor the ascension of the female virtues, and thereby these female divinities.

dess of rebirth suggest that the spiral roots of the mother-goddess cult go very deep in human history. Whether or not this goddess of the mammoth-hunters was thought to be protection against vengeful spirits, it is clear that she was associated in some way with a hope for the child's return or rebirth. In the Neolithic period, as we have seen, this constellation received a terrific burst of energy from the new idea of seed burial, and thus the new symbology was solidified: the goddess, bearer of the vengeful eye and protector against it, now encompassed as guide and as emblem all the labyrinthine passages into and out of life.

Chapter Six

The proper starting point for a Freudian anthropology is the pre-Oedipal mother. What is given by nature, in the family, is the dependence of the child on the mother. Male domination must be grasped as a secondary formation, the product of the child's revolt against the primal mother.

N. O. Brown

Wherever the mother goddess appears, in fine—and she appears either prominent or submerged throughout the known history of *Homo sapiens* from the Aurignacian caves, through the artifacts and rituals of Siberian and Alaskan hunters and primitive planters, thence to explode in the settled villages of the Near East and the Mediterranean, where she continues to animate the Catholic Madonnas of the present day—she joins to herself the two basic powers of existence: fecundity and death, birth and rebirth. In her is embodied the power of the waxing and waning moon that dies and is reborn on schedule; the power of the son-sun that plunges into the sea at night and rises reborn the next morning; the mystery of the serpent sloughing its skins endlessly, eating its own tail, getting absolutely no-where. But this matriarchal worldview does not hold center stage indefinitely. For one thing it demands acceptance of a basically static world: space condenses to matter as matter disperses again to space; light shades imperceptibly to dark as explosion shifts imperceptibly to implosion, life imperceptibly to death—with the individual of moment only as a note that recurs in a rich but redundant round. For another, it evokes continual, and in the settled planter societies, bloody sacrifice to assure that repeating melody, that continuing regeneration. Perhaps more important, conditions change, groups move, and sooner or later, one way or the other, the hunters return. The warrior-nomads return. This has probably happened more often than we know, but two occasions are noteworthy: once, as we have already seen, when the glaciers retreated and the naked mother goddess of the mammoths was displaced by the costumed shaman of the caves working his magic for the bison-hunter; and again at the threshold of the historical era. Joseph Campbell sets the Near Eastern occurrence of this latter return at the time when the early Bronze-Age civilizations such as those in Mesopotamia and Crete, with predominantly matriarchal mythologies, were being displaced; and he calls it "solarization."[46] Though the process would have been always gradual and preceded by long periods of the melding of partly nomadic (solar) and partly settled (lunar) ideologies, the term is useful here because of the suggestion it conveys of the high contrast found in direct sunlight as opposed to the softer tones of lunar, matriarchal light. Darkness, that is, flees from the sun as its opposite; whereas by moonlight, darkness and light coexist with boundaries obscured. The patriarchal view of the warriors, then, reenters as the searing eye of the sun* and sets apart all pairs of opposites—male and female, life and death, truth and falsehood, good and evil—as if they were absolutes. Once and for all. It is the second great separation.

For now in come the sons of light, the warrior pastoralists of mountain and desert, the father worshipers with their male gods, Zeus of the lightning bolt, Jahweh of the all-seeing eye. And what they do everywhere is trample and dismember the old Neolithic order of the earth, the mother goddess and her consorts and children. The Babylonian epic of Marduk, who slays and dismembers the mother goddess Tiamat (Marduk's great-great-great-grandmother), is probably the prototype. The mode of these patriarchal gods, be it Zeus defeating the Titans or Jahweh conquering Levi-

*The more one reflects, the more it appears that the changed symbolism of the eye goddess about 3400 B.C. (see page 96) represented something beyond even balance. For recall that previous manifestations of the mother goddess usually emphasized obvious feminine attributes, many of them manifestations of female fat, which are undoubtedly connected with generation and pregnancy. Indeed, it has been suggested that female fat was an evolutionary development meant to insure that even in famine times, the female would have a reserve of nourishment for her offspring. Adding to this the fact that fat was later considered by the Greeks to be the stuff of the psyche-soul (or unconscious), it may be that the transfer of godhood to the eyes of the eye goddess was a balance all right, but a precarious one, one that prefigured a coming change. For the dominance of the warrior kings of the solar eye was not far behind. And the eyes of the goddess in 3400 B.C. may have been a signal that a more fundamental change was about to take place—the change embodied by the solar warriors of keen eyesight, the change that would eventually enthrone consciousness (eyes) at the expense of the unconscious. Thus the Greek (and Hebrew) idea of soul or thymos associated with the eyes and consciousness would be the logical outgrowth of this

athan, is reversal: what was up comes down, that which was on high is thrust underground or repressed (much like the sense of smell when vision became dominant) and transformed into demon or devil or witch or Satan. To use the terms already employed, the new mythmakers split the deities of the old order into good and bad, arrogate the good to themselves and consign the bad to the underworld. So the mother goddess (and thereby everything associated with her) is split into "good mother" and "bad mother." As is the mother when the infant is weaned. Whence the good mother becomes love, life, light, the virginal Mary, mother of god, ascending to heaven. While the bad mother becomes hellish and savage—the Medusa of the snaky hair whose looks turn to stone; the lamia with removable eyes who steals children and drinks young men's blood; Eve of Genesis through whose collusion with Satan humans taste of the forbidden fruit, see in a new way, and lose paradise. Females all, they are manifestations all of the consuming tomb of the dark and bloody earth.

What comes to life in this way are the systems, both political (warrior kings of city-states) and religious (origin myths) of the Western patriarchate that is yet in power; where life, which once revolved around the suppression of the individual and his self-effacement before a communal appeasing of mysteries, now centers around bragging "big men"—chiefs or kings whose ability to sack cities and accumulate treasure redounds to the credit of their individual and political and, yes, divine lineages.[47] So that in time and inevitably these Aryan and Semite raider societies arrogate to their male sky gods (usually one) the creation of everything from nothing as the mother goddess had created in the past. Though the final step is the best known, the entire mythmaking process, according to Campbell, encompasses four steps: from the world born of a goddess without a consort; to the world born of a goddess fecundated by a consort; to the world fashioned from the body of a goddess by a male warrior god (Marduk using the body of Tiamat); to, at last, the world created by the unaided power of a male god alone (the Lord God Jehovah in the Book of Genesis creates the universe on his own in seven days). A major difference, of course, between the old mother goddess creation and the new father god creation lies in the treatment of the underside, whereby anything negative that sneaks into the patriarchal creation must be considered unwanted residue from the old system—the old fertility demons, the fallen angels, the

earlier displacement upward. The shift of iconography from female fat to female eye (of the goddess) would then have prefigured the coming shift of soul from female fat (the *omentum* of sacrifice) to male fat (brain and spinal marrow) and thence to the male solar eye of consciousness.

goddess and her consort bulls and pigs and lions and serpents, all those who must be responsible for evil, who must indeed be responsible for death itself. For no longer are life and death envisioned as equal and identical, the one continuum that brings forth endless forms both good and bad; no, life and death, and with them soul and body, are henceforth separate and separated and in continual strife; wherein the evil powers of nature (including the suppressed powers of the unconscious) must be projected outside man and god to be defamed, scapegoated, and subjugated again and again: "O Death, where is thy sting?"

Not surprisingly, the separation, this second great separation of which we in the West are the heirs, does not really work. Always the break seems a bit forced. As Campbell puts it, "the spiritual depth and interest of the myths, even of the patriarchal gods, continues to rest with the dark presences of the cursed earth."[48] Indeed it does. Witness the superior interest of the underside and its figures throughout Western history: the *Inferno* of Dante; Satan in *Paradise Lost*; Faust in Goethe's masterwork; the spell cast by Prometheus bound or unbound; the irrepressible power of the mother myth behind the Christ; and the entire span of mysticism and magic and alchemy (and their fair-haired child, science) which ever animates the Western mind, its dedication to light and progress and rationality notwithstanding. Yes, the depth and interest continue to lie behind that veil where light cannot penetrate, where vision cannot discriminate, because being itself will not reduce to light and dark, figure and ground; it will not separate into this and that, womb and tomb, me and not-me; for being and eyesight are incompatible, finally, the former irreducibly monistic, the latter by nature dualistic. So that always behind the rationally conceived, pristine statue of the Christian Madonna, there lurks the dark figure of the mother goddess, who was definitely no virgin. "*Putanna la madonna*" is the way my father typically put it: "Whore mother of God." A terrible curse word it always seemed to me, taught to venerate that immaculate conception, but to him a true reflection of his world.

That world, the world of *mal occhio*, was and still is patriarchal on the surface all right. But regularly as that curse, the split-off elements of the matriarchate would keep irrupting to color everything earthen. For it seems clear that it is those subterranean residues of mother-goddess worship, added to the preoedipal dynamics that must work here much as they do for Slovak-Americans, that together form the substrata for *mal occhio*. The threat symbolized by *mal occhio* is thus not only a projection of preoedipal rage and fear of engulfment by the retaliating mother;* it is equally a threat from the split-off earth. That is, it is a threat from the powers that combine to keep each person bound in the continuing round of generation—powers that represent not the conscious will of the perfectible, bragging individual, separated once and for all from his ground in nature and the village, but the interconnected, ever-birthing, ever-dying life of the earth. That the Italian earth still lives in this sense may be gauged by the fact that springs in some parts of southern Italy are still called *occhi*, or eyes. The name is apparently a residue of the older Greek belief that springs and pools were really the eyes of a many-eyed dragon.[50] Like *mal occhio* itself, this dragon must be one of the repressed powers of the old order that stay alive through everything.

With respect to the schema outlined by Garrison and Arensberg, moreover, the connections of *mal occhio* with the mother goddess make additional sense. For the patron most often invoked when evil eye threatens is the one symbolized by the *corno*, or horn; and the horn is preeminently the symbol of the goddess—the horn that resembles the crescent moon, the horn of her bull, the horn that suggests the phallus of her son. And here, the horned gesture seems to say not only, "Beware, this is the sign of my protector, the mother goddess," but also, "Beware, this is the sign of her son, that son whose mother can refuse him nothing, who will follow him to the underworld if necessary, that son who cannot be permanently hurt by death or the vicissitudes of this world for he rises again and again, even as the phallus, even as life." Even as the phallus, the symbol which, when united with the mother goddess, signifies regeneration and return in balance, but which, when separated off, means something else again (as indeed the axe when double belongs to the goddess, but single points to the warrior-nomads; as again the eye when paired bespeaks the goddess, but single points to *mal occhio*).

For to be sure, there is that in the phallic gesture which repudiates the mother-goddess order as well, which protests this recurring round that binds one forever on the double spiral, calling one down again and again in the dying fall. There is that which says that the forces of generation* can be tamed, controlled, and put in the service not of the paired eyes of the mother, but of that single phallic eye aiming toward flight, toward total vision, even fi-

*There is much evidence that generation, that is, procreation, represents a problem to the conscious mind for it always implies death. Alexander, for example, said that intercourse made him feel his mortality. Heraclitus said, "for souls, it is enjoyment or death to become liquid (i.e. fall into generation.)"[51] Now if we consider this "dying-fall" idea in terms of the ancient Greek concept of soul, we find that the psyche-soul, which corresponds to the unconscious, is conceived of as driven toward both generation and rage, but always unmindful of the consequences; it accepts both enjoyment and death. This appears to coincide with our own ideas about instinctual drives: they ignore consequences, even unto death. The thymos-soul, or consciousness, however, could be expected to care about the death side. For whereas the psyche was thought to persist after death, the thymos did not, as consciousness does not, as ego does not. Yet it wants to go on, the ego cannot conceive its own death. Therefore, as thymos (consciousness) becomes in time more and more the primary attribute of man, it preempts the role that originally belonged to the psyche, that is, generation, but tends to reject its concomitant, death. It seeks to erect the phallus as an icon (all puns intended), to invest it with immortality, thereby conceiving of generation without death. As related to the *mal occhio* attack —which derives from the repressed powers that include death as part of generation—the phallic gesture can thus be viewed as a consciousness-generated response symbolic of the desire for immortality.

nally penetrating (and coming out alive, with photographs) the most secret of all secrets, the mystery beneath the veil of the goddess herself—the mystery of the ultimate source and mechanism of all existence. Indeed, this is what each successive separation signifies: another attempt to achieve dominance over life, over being, by getting outside it or above it to see it better than ever, to freeze it finally and forever and separate without submitting to it, without closing with it, without dying. Love without death.

It is what the particle physicists keep hoping, is it not? That if they can somehow invent a big enough machine, with enough billions of volts, they can push particles fast enough to at last split matter (*mater*) into its irreducible elements and *see it all*. But somehow, grand as is the vision, elaborate as is the hardware, they never do. Always, there is another reflection; always another veil.

Chapter Seven

*Every will which enters into self-
hood and seeks the ground of its
life-form (sc. in itself) breaks itself
off from the mystery and enters
into a capriciousness. It cannot do
otherwise for its fellow members
stir up dying and death. It lies, and
denies union with the Will of God
and sets selfhood in its place, so
that it goes out from unity into a
desire for self. If it knew that all
things have brought it forth and
are its mothers, and if it did not
hold its mother's substance for its
own, but in common, then greed,
envy, strife, and a contrary will
would not arise.*

Boehme

*For as long as unconditional
attachment through* cupiditas
*exists, the veil is not lifted and the
heights of a consciousness free of
contents and free of illusion are not
attained; nor can any trick nor any
deceit bring this about.*

Jung

The eye, then, the eye that has gone
bad, represents a fundamental anxiety in humankind. It is the anxiety over
separation, in the first instance, from the

protection of the mother; in every instance thereafter, from situations reminiscent of that first terrible anxiety, which is fear of death. And the attack of *mal occhio* is founded in the same anxiety: those subject to attack are those who, one way or the other—by their perfection or beauty or pride or possessions—set themselves off, separate from the community of which they are a natural part. In every case *mal occhio* strikes and in so doing represents the call of the group to return, to undo the separating tendency, to reunite once more with village, family, earth.* On the other hand, the protective measures—the amulets, the cure with oil and water—seem to aim in the opposite direction. They seem to be aids, that is, not so much in returning to the fold, but in getting away with the separation, in becoming unique by means of the gesture which itself symbolizes uniqueness and separation—the phallic gesture. For the phallic gesture, in the face of the continuing claims of earth/family/community to temper that tendency to separate, continually says yes, continually counters that escape through breaking the bonds of fate is not only possible but as inevitable as the rising of the sun, of the phallus itself. So that as history, particularly Western history demonstrates, the urge from the fall onward toward separa-

*Interpretation should not be taken to mean that the fear of attack always stems from psychological, that is, self-induced causes. No, there is a reality to which *mal occhio* corresponds, regarding which a recent news article is instructive: A childless clerk of a court administering over a poor village in India contrived to have a young offender steal a three-year-old child in return for clemency. The two then sacrificed the child in a ritual designed to gain fertility for the childless

tion is continuous and inexorable: give a man a wheel or a pistol or a pesticide and he will use it. And though each separation represents another fall, another loss, it must be remembered that each is also, like the first, fortunate. Something is gained. As in the case of upright stance, visual rather than chemical sexuality was gained, and thereby not only a certain freedom from periodic compulsion, but also the undeniable richness and complexity of the social and cultural life that followed. To say nothing of consciousness. Consciousness, which the second great separation concretizes; for the elevation of the male gods, Zeus and Jahweh, can in one sense be viewed as representing the enthronement of consciousness (or ego or neocortex) and the denigration of the unconscious (or id or reptilian brain) from which it sprung. Consciousness, which is much like the vision that is its symbol: however errant, however incomplete, it is yet the necessary vehicle for comprehension, for being, that is, on a new (one yearns to say "higher," but given the loss that seems to accompany each purported advance, one hangs fire) level. To separate, then, to escape from old bonds, seems inevitable, but under what conditions? And to what end?

The end. Teleology. From the Greek word *telos*, the end. Which originally

clerk. The article concludes: "there was almost total unanimity in the village that sacrifices do work to insure conception among the childless."[52] In the face of this, can one be surprised that mothers in India once took great pains to disguise the beauty of their children, sometimes splattering them with dung, to keep them from being admired?

meant circling or band; hence the end as circle, or band. The Bahia wristband amulet against *mal ojo* invokes the protection of "Senhor do Bonfim," patron of the "good end."

The end, if universal rhythms are any guide, must be a return; and to find it, I would submit that the figure of Mercurius, that figure who for the alchemists represented the soul, or *vinculum*, or link, must be a key. Now Mercurius was an important god to the Romans, as he was to the Greeks who invented him. As the Greek Hermes, the half-Titan, he was the link between the old reptilian order and the new solar order of Olympians. He was the messenger of the gods, the go-between on errands between heaven and earth, as well as between earth and the underworld. He it was who led Odysseus on his journey, protected him from dangerous mother-goddess manifestations such as Circe and Nausicaa so that they in turn could protect him on his descent into the underworld, and led him, finally, home to Penelope. He is the original of the guide who in a later manifestation as Vergil leads Dante safely through his tour of the underworld.

This is not to say that the qualities of Hermes or Mercury are all benign. The bringer of increase and thereby wealth, he is also the thief, the trickster, the go-between who is also a pander. Joseph Campbell links him in his trickster role with

the chief mythological character of the Paleolithic world of story. A fool and a cruel, lecherous cheat, an epitome of the principle of disorder, he is nevertheless the culture-bringer also. . . . Among the Greeks he was Hermes, the shape-shifter and master of the way to the land of the dead, as well as Prometheus, the fire-bringer.[53]

At one of his festivals on Samos, called the feast of Hermes Charidotes, we are told that "the populace was allowed to steal and to commit highway robbery."[54] In even older manifestations, this shape-shifting guide and traducer of men was imaged phallically as the Herm, the masculine principle and generative force of life. He was the ithyphallic god who led souls (psyches) away at death and led them back again from the underworld at birth. He was a mediator between two worlds who "conjures up the new creation."[55]

To the alchemists the Spirit Mercurius had these same qualities: many-faceted, contradictory, he could be cold fire as well as water; the revelatory light of nature as well as the stinking water, *aqua foetida*; a dragon as well as the soul of the world. Jung points out that he seems to be divine as well as human, and in this he is compared to Christ: "he calls to mind that double figure which seems to stand behind both Christ and the devil . . . that enigmatic Lucifer whose attributes are shared by both."[56] Both old and young, he is both Hermes senex, the old man "attested to by archeology [which] brings him into direct relationship with Saturn," and the divine child.[57] As Saturn was elsewhere considered to be the father of Mercury, it becomes legitimate to think of Mercurius as that being who is both father and son, that being who, *causa sui*, can beget himself. He is, in short, both male and female, good and evil, the pure masculine principle as well as the androgyne, the hermaphroditic principle of life prior to differentiation. Jung, indeed, would have it that Mercurius, in this undifferentiated aspect, represents the unconscious from which all differentiations spring.

In Roman Italy, Mercury's connection to Saturn and thereby to the Italian Golden Age makes him a notable figure in another respect. For the Saturnalia, that festival which in Rome belonged to Saturn but in Samos, as noted above, was dedicated directly to Hermes, was a festival of reversal. The established order was overturned; slaves could order about their masters, and all restraints could be overthrown. The outsiders in effect ruled. The Saturnalia was in part, then, a turning of

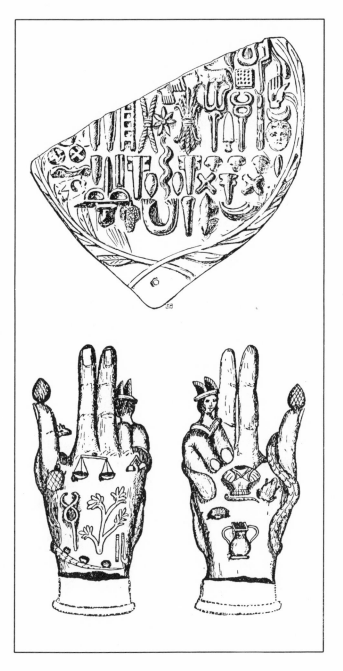

Mercury's importance as a divinity in Italy can be further deduced from several areas of evidence. As Hermes, he is found on Etruscan mirrors and is called *turms aitas*, "Hermes of Hades," an expression that emphasizes his chthonic and dual aspect as Hades-Hermes, Kabeirian father and son.[58] Further, his presence is found in great numbers on the votive objects described by Elworthy in *Horns of Honour*. While these hands and *dischi sacri* contain a complex agglomeration of symbols, the appearance of the caduceus, the serpent, the frog, the cock, the ram's head, and the turtle, symbols all of Mercurius, suggest that he has been a favorite god of the populace throughout Italian history.

the world upside down, an invasion from below of the seemingly powerless. Now if we recall that in the evil-eye event in all cultures it is the outsider who is most generally considered responsible for the attacks (monks, priests, widows, the Indian class in Mexico, the Buda among the Amhara), it follows that the *mal occhio* event in one sense parallels the Saturnalia. For in both, the corrective to a world in which some have more than others or seek to have more, is the attack from below, the attack from the outsiders. *Mal occhio* is an attack from the repressed or spurned powers of balance, of equality; the Saturnalia is a reversion of the unequal but established order by the repressed of society. And Mercurius is related to both.

A legitimate question, of course, arises. For if Mercurius does indeed figure as part of the upwelling threat of *mal occhio* (and the underworld and mother), then how are we to understand his other aspect in the event, wherein he corresponds to the phallic principle, the generative force and seed of nature which is counterpoised to the threat of *mal occhio* from below? That is, how can Mercurius represent both attack and response; how can he be both good and evil?

The answer to the first part of the question involves the paradoxical nature of the god—and indeed of the mother goddess herself, who also figures in both ends of the *mal occhio* event. For both deities are at once whole and partial. Mercurius is both father and son, both Titan and Olympian, both Herm and hermaphrodite; the mother goddess likewise manifests as both "primal one and only," sufficient unto herself, and as differentiated pair with her consort-son. This being the case, the *mal occhio* attack, as suggested, derives from that whole aspect below all right, but in a form that may *appear partial**** (that is, differentiated, as the mother image appears split or partial to the infant), as either the devouring feminine eye or the penetrating masculine eye. The response evoked in opposition, therefore, is likewise partial: the *corno* amulet that can be the sign of either the goddess or her son.

The answer to the second part of the question involves no less a paradox than the first, than the fortunate fall, than the nature of any process that "begins with evil and ends with good" (such as the primeval soup of a lifeless planet that leads to man, or the body of fallen man that leads to a Christ or soul). That is to say, the *mal occhio* attack itself may partake of a paradoxical fortunate-fall quality via this god who brings both death and life, both sickness and health, both seizure and wealth.

*Iconographically, the two eyes of the goddess can appear as one when they are capped by eyebrows that meet to suggest one eyebrow and hence one eye. This links up with the belief in evil-eye cultures that people whose eyebrows grow together into one are widely believed to have evil eye.

In the Hermes hymn, for example, we are shown a being who indifferently slaughters an innocent turtle, and then makes a divine lyre of its shell; killing and music, good and evil are inextricably mixed. Indeed, we have already seen this Mercurial action at work in the *mal occhio* event, where the threat of evil borne by the eye operates to keep village society more or less equal—as in Morocco, where if a person admires another's possession, the possessor will sooner or later insist that the admirer accept it as a gift. The threat of evil eye thus acts in a way that encourages generosity, an undeniable social good.

There is another, less apparently pragmatic level to this good/evil strand, moreover. It is a level whose main referent is personal—my childhood experiences with *mal occhio*, which, it may be remembered, invariably led to those fevers wherein the dominant sense was one of being merged with the objects that surrounded and overwhelmed me:

it is going back again. everything is getting smaller again like a balloon losing air except not really emptying like a balloon into space, no, pouring out of me and back into their own things.

Now there has always seemed to me to be something implicit in those *mal occhio* attacks, something that bore intimations beyond the apparently malign, frightening facts. I mean intimations of some other mode of apprehension that lay always just out of reach of me; me seeing myself both one with and apart from the current that had me; me both terrified of that imminent annihilation and fascinated that I was it, this cleavage and boundary of which I was both, both of it and above it. Often the taste of it would return to electrify my teeth for days. And it intimated something, that sickness, which breakdown often enough portends—shaman sickness, for instance, whereby entry to a vision or a power or a sacred song is won. That the message was always cut off, that the malady was turned back by Zi' Carmela's appeal to the curative powers, or before it even began, by the prophylactic gesture, may simply mean that such things are fated to remain always a bit beyond one's grasp. On the other hand, once taste of that other, that awesomely inclusive mode and one cannot help wondering if the cutoff by cure or gesture might not be considered in another way—a way that depends on the illusory double or even triple nature of Mercurius.

For it must not be forgotten that Mercurius is a trickster, a traducer. Just as vision is a traducer, leading one to believe in forms whose ultimate reality is by no means secure. Just as the phallus, the geni-

Three-legged Mercury from Fortunio Liceto's *De Lucernis*, 1652.

{137}

tal organization itself, is a traducer, leading one to invest all one's libido in genitality, when at heart what is yearned for is a more complete loving, a more complete union:

The natural function of the ego, as Freud says in *The Ego and the Id*, is to be the sensitive surface of the entire body; but the survival of *causa sui* fantasies attached to the genital establishes in the unconscious, as Ferenczi said, the phallus as a miniature of the total ego.[59]

Phallus and ego. Phallus and ego and eye. Phallus and ego and eye and soul. There is always more, and less, than appears. But some mind-set like the following may be critical: Mercurius as phallus, the phallus as miniature ego (that is, the generative force preempted by the male sex, placed exclusively in the genital and made willful, which is to say conscious and egoic) is always a trickster, always illusory. Just as the eye is a trickster. Just as the projections that derive from the temporary separation of the world into good mother and bad mother lead to the exaggerated belief in evil outside and good inside; good me and envious them; virgin-wife/mother and whore/all-other-women. Traducers all, they are tricksters all, just as is the psychic separation that all represent—the separation of mental life into consciousness/rationality/good at war with unconscious/

irrationality/bad. All in every case are partial—the traductions of the shape-shifter Mercurius. Yet in every case they are also inevitable. And necessary. Not only in the sense that they make possible functioning in the world as it is—recall the child-stealers—but also in the larger sense that only by separation, only by the hero's being cut off from the bonds of home and mother and forced to follow each *ignis fatuus* through the enthusiasms and tragedies and stupidities of life can he ultimately return, and with new eyes. With new eyes, for the fall is always in some sense fortunate.

The attack from below, then, the attack of *mal occhio* does indeed intimate a message from that subterranean ground of consciousness that Mercurius represents: "Everywhere that Hermes appears, even when it is as 'guardian,' there is an influx and invasion from the underworld."[60] It is a message that portends unbinding, a message that portends indeed that ancient prophecy of unbinding the trickster Prometheus himself: "One day his chains will fall away of themselves and the world-eon of Zeus will dissolve."[61] While this suggests a death (Nietzsche's death of god?), we can guess that like all unbindings* it points beyond itself to something more, to some new binding, some new and divine

*R. B. Onians, in *The Origins of European Thought*, points out that in Greek mystery religions such as the Orphic mysteries, unbinding was regularly a prelude to a new binding on another level. The belt binding one to one's old destiny on earth—the confinements of family, polis, fate, and the body itself—was removed and replaced by a new band. The new binding clearly symbolized another, and superior, *telos*.

connubium of above with below, of dark with light, of all the separated-off elements of the mother-goddess order with their conqueror—to the union, in fine, of the Olympian Mercury with the power from which he derives, that old Titan self which is "older, greater, and stronger than the gods."[62] What this may mean in actual terms—that is, what the rough beast might be that Yeats predicted was "slouching toward Bethlehem to be born"—cannot be easily defined or divined. But in psychic terms, at least, some hints have been given. For if Zeus and his Olympians represent the separated and separating ego, and the dethroned Titans and mother goddesses the suppressed id, then the intimated union would approximate that psychic one insisted upon by Jung: the project of every modern human is to make the unconscious conscious, is to reunite as far as possible with all the unconscious contents which humans have been denying these last three thousand years. This would amount to the recall of all those projections both evil and good—projections analogous to the one which animates *mal occhio* by envisioning evil eyes and envy "out there" when in fact they reside mainly within— which have threatened to make the twentieth century, with its scapegoats in the concentration camps and gulags, the century of mass projection and thereby mass murder.

The intimated union need not be stated in purely Jungian terms, however, for the Freudian schema implies something similar. And in those terms, as elucidated by Norman O. Brown, one might predict a union that would move toward ending what has been called the "tyranny of genital organization." By this is meant that exclusive concentration of libido or energy in the genital, a concentration made compulsive by anxiety and fear of death, which is ultimately the fear of separation from the protecting mother; and which by a paradoxical reaction leads to the fantastic project to become "independent of the totality conceived of as the mother principle."[63] It is a tyranny that eventuates in "super-organic" culture, which by definition alienates its members from the organic ground that gave them birth—and if there is anything that typifies modern culture, it is certainly alienation from the ground which it flies over and rolls over and chemicalizes over and paves over in its vain attempt not to touch it, not to die. It is a tyranny wholly acceptable, however, only to the conscious ego and its symbolic analogues, phallus/ego/eye. For the unconscious, if the great body of analytical material can be believed, rejects this genital tyranny—"mankind is unalterably in the unconscious, in revolt against sexual differentiation and genital organization"[64] —just as it earlier rejected the fact of differentiation and thereby separation from the mother. Just as Catholic Italy and Mexico earlier resisted separation from mother-goddess worship, hence the cult of the Virgin. Just as village cultures with their cyclical agrarian rhythms early resisted total submersion in the more linear rhythms of the pastoralists, hence *mal occhio*. No, the unconscious resists, the unconscious yearns always for the old project, the old sense of interdependent, multifaceted union with the world, with the mother. But —and it is a huge but—such a union, if it can even be conceived, would have to be of a fundamentally different kind than that once envisioned in infantile fantasies (that is, the re-union of child body with mother body, a fantasy that differentiation and the castration complex render forever impossible). It would have to be a reunion that did not violate the terms of the taboo. The veil.

The veil. It is no accident that we are back. To the same wall hit previously. The same wall and I think the same taboo, that primal taboo that involves differentiating vision and thereby *cupiditas*—eyes that desire. Whose corollary is that the ultimate union must involve *vision without cupiditas*: "for as long as unconditional attachment through *cupiditas* exists, the veil is not lifted."[65] That is to say, as long as the tyrannies—the genital, the egoic, the visual—continue to dominate life, there will continue to exist conscious desire and the veil, separation and dualism: "the dualism of self and other, the dualism which infantile fantasies had sought to overcome."[66] The words are those of Norman O.Brown, but they could as well be those of a Zenist. Or a computer scientist whose work with artificial intelligence convinces him in a quite concrete way that the old paradox that overrides (or undergirds) all others is the attempt of intelligence to include itself in its own system. The problem reduces to the frustrating fact that no system can be its own metasystem; that which looks (at itself) remains always outside that which is being looked at (itself), thereby making of the object in question (itself) a forever receding, always partial, mirage. As G. Spencer Brown points out, the objective reality we see is by definition incomplete: "Its particularity is the price we pay for its visibility."[67] The veil is not lifted.

Yet to lift it, to see the goddess without desire, without envy, without the intermediary of all the false projections that originate within the separating tendencies of ego/eye/phallus, is the demand. How can this be understood? or brought about? Must one, after all, go blind like Tiresias?

If it knew that all things have brought it forth and are its mothers, and if it did not hold its mother's substance for its own, but in common . . .

These words of the mystic Jakob Boehme appear to offer a way out, or in, or at least a clue thereto. It is a clue found in every return after every fall, in each reunion that follows each separation. A clue that suggests that the return must be made on broader ground and with wider visual scope than pure self-regard can provide. A clue that suggests that some more radical unbinding, some absolute separation from the single and dominant mother that inspires envy and *cupiditas* may in fact be the precondition to a return to mothers beyond number. "The Mothers!" cries Faust before he sinks to them. For as long as the human mind clings to its idea of self as locally determined, as bound to one place, one ego, one mother, family, village, separate from all others, then it cannot help but erect all the false projects, all the genital projects and projections that follow the traducer Mercurius again and again down the path of subjugating and then repossessing the one mother (or her substitutes in endless series) as object. Don Juan is his own hell. In Italy, as in all cultures to a greater or lesser degree, sublimated as rockets or magic or nuclear accelerators or the myriad forms of seductive exploitation, this is the fundamental error. It is a flight from death into the arms of successive mothers.

If, on the other hand, the human mind can once realize—and the realization is quite distinct from the intellectual conception which is ego-driven; for the realization involves a death, either of the ego or of the projects to which it is bound—if it can at last realize that *all things are its mothers*, all earth, all life, all time, all trees (evolutionary theory is perhaps the grandest testament to this idea, but despite its use of a mother tree as schema, one does not *feel* the truth of it; one thinks the truth and yet feels separate); then its compulsive desires, envy of others, projections, separations of reality into this and that, me and not-me, might be suddenly rendered transparent, invert, empty. And it might see, and not with the single eye of envy or even the double eyes of balance, but with the full perception of its entire sensory and extrasensory apparatus, what its own science is even now saying: that all differentiations—wave-particle, masculine-feminine, psyche-thymos, consciousness-un-

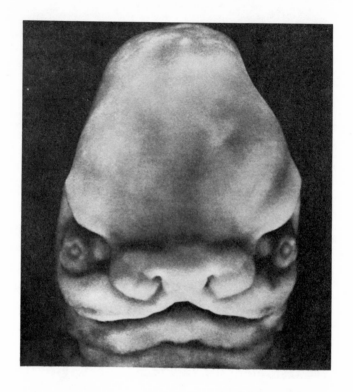

Face of a forty-day-old human embryo. The uncanny feeling one gets from this photograph may derive from the fact that as humans are said to have evolved via neoteny—the retention of some embryonic or immature characteristics into adulthood—the image here may be a window into both past and future.

consciousness, life-death—all spring from the same fundamental fire, that all connective and reflective fire that is coterminous with itself, of itself, that is, in the old Zen phrase, "its face before it was born." It might see, in a word, that it is the androgyne. With nothing to possess. That it embodies, like a fully manifested Mercurius, both self and the ground from which it came. Its reunion then with that maternal matrix which is itself becomes as inevitable as the separations which prepared its way.

Now it is clear that the language one uses

to express such a view may be categorized as mystical. But perhaps the pejorative loses force if one considers, as Norman O. Brown did years ago, that:

Freud's exploitation of the myth of the primal hermaphrodite or androgyne shows [that] psychoanalysis, interpreted as a phenomenon in the history of human thought, is only an interpretation of the dreams of mysticism.[68]

And what that mysticism (that is, the deep and as yet unsatisfied longings of the human spirit) seems to have always held central is the myth of the androgyne:

According to this idea, to God's conception of him, man is a complete, masculinely feminine being, solar and telluric, logoic and cosmic at the same time. . . . Original sin is connected in the first instance with the division into two sexes and the Fall of the androgyne, i.e. of man as a complete being.[69]

To the complete being, then, the return is to the community conceived in its broadest possible terms. Though this does not quite express the whole of it either; the complete being, whatever he or she might appear to be, is already returned.

To be sure, this is not to say that in Italy, or in Italian America, the attack of *mal occhio* bears this message to all who believe in it. Rather, one would guess that the more familiar aspect of Mercurius holds the field, Mercurius as the

Kabeirian guide of souls ... [who] guides souls out of his realm—the world of paths and roads—back into the warm life of the household, which in Greek signifies "family."[70]

Yes, the *mal occhio* attack would express that to the Italian—a guiding of the errant soul, the soul perhaps grown too proud or independent or alienated, back into the warm life of the family which has always, through every invasion from either without or within, sustained him. As Hermes once led Odysseus across all waters, through hell and successive mothers, back to hearth and home and earthly connubium with Penelope. In Greek, not incidentally, married union is a restoration of the primal condition; and so the married couple is referred to as "*to androgyno*, the androgene."[71]

Still, even in Italy—where the family in any case is not what it once was—one gets the suspicion that more than family, more than mother upon whom family depends, more than the old bonds that fester in Italian families no less than elsewhere must be implied by *mal occhio*. One suspects, that is, that where the concept of soul is involved, and where the words "soul," "seed," and "phallus" all spring from a common source—which brings to mind the fact that Mercury was the god of springs (a source) as well, relating him to

{148}

the word for spring in southern Italy, *occhi*, or eyes—there, too, will be intimated, consciously or not, some sense of that return to a more ubiquitous mother than the one normally visualized. For the corollary to the highly evolved visual sense one finds in things Italian, the underside of that love of surface, is the intuition of its evanescence: where fullness is will sooner or later be emptiness. And this emptiness, too, has its beauty of expression:

There is an inherent Mediterranean austerity much in evidence in the Naples area, in Sorrento and Capri, which seems to come from the sea, since it is hardly to be found inland. This expresses itself in a taste for unadorned spaces, and is the visual equivalent of intervals of silence.[72]

I like those "intervals of silence." They make me think of Pirandello plays on the illusory nature of fact. They make me think of unfinished statues by Michelangelo. They make me think of spirals incised in stone. They make me think that alongside the familiar and familial binding in *mal occhio*, there must equally exist that other, that subterranean intimation: that all Mercurial phenomena—the visual, the phallic, the egoic—are at some stage to be unbound or unwound, to yield at last to that more complete, that more all-embracing vision.

REFERENCES

1. Quoted by Edward S. Gifford, Jr., *The Evil Eye: Studies in the Folklore of Vision* (New York: Macmillan Co., 1958), p. 17.
2. Willa Appel, "The Myth of the Jettatura," *The Evil Eye*, ed. Clarence Maloney (New York: Columbia University Press, 1976), pp. 16–27.
3. Phyllis H. Williams, *South Italian Folkways in Europe and America* (New Haven: Yale University Press, 1938), p. 156.
4. Ibid., p. 178.
5. Richard Swiderski, "From Folk to Popular: Plastic Evil Eye Charms," *The Evil Eye*, ed. Clarence Maloney (New York: Columbia University Press, 1976), pp. 29–41.
6. Alan Dundes, *Interpreting Folklore*, "Wet and Dry, the Evil Eye: An Essay in Indo-European and Semitic Worldview" (Bloomington: University of Indiana Press, 1980), pp. 93–133.
7. Carl Jung, *The Psychology of the Transference* (Princeton: Bollingen Series, 1969), p. 80.
8. Ibid., p. 82.
9. Ibid., p. 84.
10. Ibid., p. 82.
11. Regina Dionisopoulos-Mass, "The Evil Eye and Bewitchment in a Peasant Village," *The Evil Eye*, ed. Clarency Maloney (New York: Columbia University Press, 1976), pp. 42–62.
12. Howard F. Stein, "Envy and the Evil Eye: An Essay in the Psychological Ontogeny of Belief and Ritual," *The Evil Eye*, ed. Clarence Maloney (New York: Columbia University Press, 1976), pp. 192–222.
13. Ibid., p. 198.
14. Ibid., p. 207.

15. Ibid., p. 208.
16. Ibid., p. 215.
17. Frederick Elworthy, "The Evil Eye," *Encyclopedia of Religion and Ethics*, vol. 5 (New York: Charles Scribner's Sons, 1912), pp. 608–15.
18. Vivian Garrison and Conrad M. Arensberg, "The Evil Eye: Envy or Risk of Seizure? Paranoia or Patronal Dependency?" *The Evil Eye*, ed. Clarence Maloney (New York: Columbia University Press, 1976), pp. 287–328.
19. Sigmund Freud, *Civilization and Its Discontents* (New York: Norton Paperback, 1961), p. 46.
20. Joan Erikson, "Eye to Eye," *The Man-Made Object*, ed. Gyorgy Kepes (New York: Braziller, 1966), p. 58.
21. Christopher Hills, as quoted in Allen, Bearne, and Smith, *Energy, Matter & Form* (Boulder Creek, Ca.: University of Trees Press, 1977), p. 97.
22. Garrison and Arensberg, "The Evil Eye: Envy or Risk of Seizure?" p. 306.
23. Ronald A. Reminick, "The Evil Eye Belief Among the Amhara," *The Evil Eye*, ed. Clarence Maloney (New York: Columbia University Press, 1976), p. 91.
24. Vasco Ronchi, as quoted in Allen, Bearne, and Smith, *Energy, Matter & Form*, pp. 95–100.
25. Sir James Frazer, *The New Golden Bough*, revised and edited by Theodore H. Gaster (New York: Mentor Paperback, 1959), pp. 187–204.
26. Ibid., p. 197.
27. Richard Broxton Onians, *The Origins of European Thought* (Cambridge, 1951).
28. Ibid., p. 75.
29. Ibid., p. 224.
30. Ibid., p. 252.
31. Wilhelm Wundt, *Elements of Folk Psychology* (New York: Macmillan Co., 1916), p. 228.
32. Onians, *The Origins of European Thought*, p. 109.

33. Tacitus, *Germania*, as quoted in Joseph Campbell, *The Masks of God: Occidental Mythology* (New York: Viking Press, 1964), p. 475.
34. Matthew, 5:28–29.
35. G. Spencer Brown, *Laws of Form* (London: Allen and Unwin, 1969), pp. 105–6.
36. Campbell, *The Masks of God: Occidental Mythology*, p. 64.
37. Ibid., p. 25.
38. Joseph Campbell, *The Masks of God: Primitive Mythology* (New York: Viking Press, 1959), p. 171.
39. M. E. L. Mallowan, "On Tell Brak," *Iraq*, vol. IX (2), 1947, pp. 198–210.
40. Edward Westermarck, *Ritual and Belief in Morocco*, vol. 1 (New Hyde Park, N.Y.: University Books, 1968), p. 489.
41. Samuel N. Kramer, *From the Poetry of Sumer* (Berkeley and Los Angeles: University of California Press, 1979), pp. 85–88.
42. O. G. S. Crawford, *The Eye Goddess* (London: Phoenix House, 1957).
43. Leon Stover and Bruce Kraig, *Stonehenge: The Indo-European Heritage* (Chicago: Nelson-Hall 1978), p. 111.
44. Frederick Elworthy, *Horns of Honour* (London: J. Murray, 1900), p. 71.
45. Campbell, *The Masks of God: Primitive Mythology*, p. 341.
46. Campbell, *The Masks of God: Occidental Mythology*, p. 75.
47. Stover and Kraig, *Stonehenge: The Indo-European Heritage*, pp. 130 ff.
48. Campbell, *The Masks of God: Occidental Mythology*, p. 92.
49. Norman O. Brown, *Life Against Death* (New York: Vintage Paperback, 1959), p. 114.
50. Richard Gambino, *Blood of My Blood: The Dilemma of the Italian-Americans* (New York: Anchor Paperback, 1974), p. 214.

51. Onians, *The Origins of European Thought*, p. 109.
52. "When TV Comes to Poor Villagers," *San Francisco Chronicle*, 2 August 1980.
53. Campbell, *The Masks of God: Primitive Mythology*, pp. 273, 276.
54. Karl Kerenyi, *Hermes Guide of Souls*, trans. Murray Stein (Zurich: Spring Publications, 1976), p. 84.
55. Ibid., p. 77.
56. Carl Jung, "The Spirit Mercurius," *Collected Works*, vol. 13 (New York: Pantheon, 1953–79), p. 222.
57. Ibid., p. 220.
58. Kerenyi, *Hermes Guide of Souls*, p. 80.
59. Norman O. Brown, *Life Against Death*, p. 128.
60. Kerenyi, *Hermes Guide of Souls*, p. 85.
61. Campbell, *The Masks of God: Primitive Mythology*, p. 280.
62. Ibid.
63. Norman O. Brown, *Life Against Death*, p. 130.
64. Ibid., p. 132.
65. Jung, "The Spirit Mercurius," p. 138.
66. Norman O. Brown, *Life Against Death*, p. 129.
67. G. Spencer Brown, *Laws of Form*, p. 106.
68. Norman O. Brown, *Life Against Death*, p. 133.
69. Ibid.
70. Kerenyi, *Hermes Guide of Souls*, p. 84.
71. Ibid., p. 85.
72. Norman Lewis, *Naples '44* (New York: Pantheon, 1978), p. 204.

ILLUSTRATION CREDITS

Acknowledgment is gratefully made to the following for permission to use photographs, drawings, and reproductions:

Cover: Eyes on Sumerian seal-impression of the 3rd millennium B.C. Courtesy of the Oriental Institute, The University of Chicago.

Title page: Eye-idol from Tell Brak, c. 4th millennium B.C. Courtesy of The British Museum, London.

Half title: *Cimaruta* amulet, Italian, origin unknown, possibly Naples. Courtesy of Museo Nazionale Delle Arti E Tradizioni Popolari, Rome.

Pages 27, 28: *Corno* amulets in gold and silver. Photo: Dan DeWilde.

Page 38: Homemade amulet from Brazil. Photo: Dan DeWilde.

Page 41: *Il gobbo* amulet. Photo: Dan DeWilde.

Page 42: *Cimaruta* and siren amulets, Italian, origin unknown, possibly Naples. Courtesy of Museo Nazionale Delle Arti E Tradizioni Popolari, Rome.

Page 43: Contemporary plastic amulets. *Mano cornuta* amulet. Photos: Dan DeWilde.

Page 44: *Mano fica* amulets, all from Brazil. Photo: Dan DeWilde.

Page 51: Greek Olpe from Orvieto, Italy, c. 6th century B.C. Courtesy of Lowie Museum of Anthropology, University of California, Berkeley.

Page 60: Silver siren amulet and frog amulet, both from *Naples in the Nineties*, by E. Neville-Rolfe (London: 1897). Drawings: Lawrence E. DiStasi.

Page 76: *Ojo de venado*, or "deer's eye" amulet. Photo: Dan DeWilde.

Page 78: Syrian eye-charm collected by Paul Copeland. Courtesy of Pitt-Rivers Museum, Oxford. "*Bonfim*" wristband amulet. Photo: Dan DeWilde.

Page 84: Medusa head of terra cotta, Greece, mid-6th century B.C. Courtesy of the Metropolitan Museum of Art, Harris Brisbane Dick Fund, 1939.

Page 88: Diana of Ephesus, from Agustin Calmet, *The Great Dictionary of the Holy Bible* (Charlestown, 1813).

Page 89: Mercury detail, bronze attributed to Adriaen de Vries, c. 1603. Courtesy of the National Gallery of Art, Washington, D.C. Andrew Mellon Collection.

Page 93: Head of Medusa, North Italian coin, late 15th or early 16th century. Courtesy of the National Gallery of Art. Samuel H. Kress Collection. Gorgoneum inside Attic black-figure eye-cup, Greece, 6th century B.C. Courtesy of Lowie Museum of Anthropology, University of California, Berkeley.

Page 95: Eyes on Sumerian seal-impression of the 3rd millennium B.C. Courtesy of the Oriental Institute, The University of Chicago. Eye-idols from Tell Brak, c. 4th millennium B.C., drawings after Mallowan. From *Iraq*, vol. IX. Courtesy of the British School of Archaeology in Iraq. Moroccan eyebrow designs after Edward Westermarck, *Ritual and Belief in Morocco*, vol. 1 (London: Macmillan, 1926).

Page 96: Clay goddess, Thrace (Bulgaria), Neolithic. Courtesy of Naturhistorisches Museum, Vienna.

Page 97: Stone rosette from the Eye Temple, Tell Brak, c. 4th millennium B.C. From *Iraq*, vol. IX. Courtesy of the British School of Archaeology in Iraq. Rosette amulet in silver from Morocco after Edward Westermarck, *Ritual and Belief in Morocco*, vol. 1 (London: Macmillan, 1926).

Page 100: Face-pot from Tell Hassuna, c. 1500 B.C., from O.G.S. Crawford, *The Eye Goddess* (after Mallowan in *Iraq*, vol. IX). By permission of J. M. Dent & Sons Ltd.

Page 101: Oculi at entrance to the temple of Hal Tarxien, Malta, 2400 to 2300 B.C. Courtesy of Malta Tourist Office, London.

Page 102: Eyes on Spanish pots, bones, and stones; and plaques from Portugal and Spain, from O.G.S. Crawford, *The Eye Goddess*. By permission of J. M. Dent & Sons Ltd.

Page 105: Kerbstone 52 and Entrance stone, New-grange, Ireland. Photos by Jean McMann, *Riddles of the Stone Age* (London: Thames & Hudson, 1980).

Page 106: Gavr Inis, Knockmany and Calderstones drawings, all from O. G. S. Crawford, *The Eye Goddess*. By permission of J. M. Dent & Sons Ltd. Stone goddess, St.-Sernin, southern France, per-haps late Neolithic. Courtesy of Archaeological Museum, Rodez, France. Photo: Louis Balsan.

Page 108: Bronze spectacle fibula, Greece, 10th cen-tury B.C. Courtesy of the Metropolitan Museum of Art, Fletcher Fund, 1937.

Page 115: Venus of Lespugue, ivory, Haute Ga-ronne, France, Paleolithic. Collection Musee de l'Homme, Paris.

Page 133: Votive hand and *disco sacro*, both from *Horns of Honour* by Frederick Elworthy (Lon-don: 1900).

Page 137: Mercurius triceps, from *De Lucernis* by Fortunio Liceto, 1652. Courtesy of The Bancroft Library, University of California, Berkeley. Hand of Fatima and hand figures, all from Ed-ward Westermarck, *Ritual and Belief in Morocco*, vol. 1 (London: Macmillan, 1926).

Page 146: Face of a human embryo at approximately forty days. From *The Feminine*, by Miriam and Jose Arguelles, *The Stages of Human Develop-ment Before Birth*, E. Blechschmidt. By permis-sion of E. W. B. Saunders Co., Philadelphia, 1961.

Page 151: *Cimaruta* amulet, Italian, origin un-known, possibly Naples. Courtesy of Museo Na-zionale Delle Arti E Tradizioni Popolari, Rome.